HOW I BECAME A MEMBER OF THE HUSKER FAMILY

A Memoir

How I Became a Member of the Husker Family

JAMES BROWN

Published by JAMES BROWN, 2024.

While every precaution has been taken in the preparation of this book, the publisher assumes no responsibility for errors or omissions, or for damages resulting from the use of the information contained herein.

HOW I BECAME A MEMBER OF THE HUSKER FAMILY

First edition. October 27, 2024.

Copyright © 2024 JAMES BROWN.

ISBN: 979-8227005830

Written by JAMES BROWN.

Dedication

To all the Husker family, especially the football players from 1958 to 1961. Thank you for helping me get through the University of Nebraska with a degree.

James Brown

COPYRIGHT © 2024 JAMES BROWN

All rights reserved.

HOW I BECAME A MEMBER OF THE HUSKER FAMILY: A Memoir

No part of this book may be reproduced, or stored in a retrieval system, or transmitted in any form or by any means, electronic, mechanical, photocopying, recording, or otherwise, without express written permission of the author.

Disclaimer: I have tried to recreate events, locales, and conversations from my memories of them. To protect privacy, in some instances I have changed the names of individuals and places. I may have changed some identifying characteristics and details, such as physical properties, occupations, and places of residence.

Although the author has made every effort to ensure that the information in this book was correct at the time of publication, the author does not assume and hereby disclaims any liability to any party for any loss, damage, or disruption caused by errors or omissions, whether such errors or omissions result from negligence, accident, or any other cause.

Dedication

To all the Husker family, especially the football players from 1958 to 1961. Thank you for helping me get through the University of Nebraska with a degree.

Chapter 1: An Orphan's Journey to the Heart of Nebraska Football

The roar of the crowd was deafening, but in that moment, all I could hear was my own heartbeat. I stood at the edge of the field, my hands trembling as I clutched the water bottles. This wasn't just any field—it was Memorial Stadium, home of the Nebraska Huskers. How did an orphan from Lexington High end up here, you might ask? Well, that's a story of chance, perseverance, and the power of being in the right place at the right time.

My journey began in the humble corridors of Lexington High School. As the water boy, football boy, and cage boy, I was the unsung hero of our athletic department. While the star players basked in the glory of touchdowns and stopping opponents from scoring, I was busy collecting sweaty socks and jocks, ensuring our athletes had clean gear for their next battle. It lacked glamor, but it provided my entry into a world I had only imagined joining.

Little did I know that fate had other plans for me. Our football team was on fire that year, clinching the state championship and catapulting us into the limelight. One name stood out—Monte Kiffin, our very own triple-threat superstar. As the dust settled on our victory, colleges came knocking, their eyes set on the prize that was Monte Kiffin, Mick Tinglehoff, and Dallas Dyer, along with Steve Smith, our quarterback.

The pivotal moment came during the state basketball tournament at the University of Nebraska's coliseum. There I was, proudly wearing my letter jacket—a symbol of my dedication as a student manager—when Monte's voice cut through the air.

"Who wants to go with me to see the coach?" he asked.

The silence that followed was deafening. Before I knew it, Monte had grabbed me by the sleeve, and we were off to meet the legendary Coach Bill Jennings.

As we stepped into that office, my heart raced. I felt like an imposter, a mere water boy in the presence of greatness. But then, something magical happened. Coach Jennings looked at me, really looked at me, and saw potential of winning with Monte signing with the University, where others might have seen nothing. With a simple phone call, he opened a door I never knew existed—a chance to explore the world of athletic training under the guidance of Paul Schneider, the Huskers' head trainer.

I found myself navigating the sprawling Nebraska campus after the coach give me directions for getting to the training room, my feet carrying me toward the iconic stadium. As I pushed open that red door and stepped into the locker room, I couldn't help but feel I was stepping into my destiny. The smell of liniment and determination filled my nostrils, and I knew I was home.

Paul Schneider, with his no-nonsense demeanor and wealth of knowledge, showed me a world beyond water bottles and laundry baskets. As he guided me through the training room, explaining the intricacies of ultrasound machines and rehabilitation techniques, I felt a spark ignite within me. This offered more than just a tour behind the scenes. It was the beginning of a journey that would transform me from an orphan with limited prospects to a member of the revered Husker family.

As I made my way back to the coliseum, my mind was reeling with possibilities. The basketball game continued, but I was no longer just a spectator. I was a young man with a vision, standing on the precipice of a future I never dared to imagine. The Huskers had opened their arms to me, and I was ready to embrace my new family with everything I had.

Chapter 2: The Unexpected Letter

The summer sun beat down on Lexington, Nebraska, as I trudged home from another long day of work. Thoughts of the upcoming fall and the uncertainty that lay ahead filled my mind as I spent three hours mowing Mary Diefenback's lawn. That's when I saw it—a crisp white envelope peeking out of our mailbox, bearing the unmistakable seal of the University of Nebraska Athletic Department.

My heart raced as I tore open the envelope, my fingers trembling slightly. The words on the page blurred before my eyes, but one sentence stood out clear as day: "We would like you to come this August with Monte to become a student trainer in the training room this fall."

I blinked; sure I must be dreaming. Me? A student trainer for the Huskers? It seemed too good to be true.

George Sullivan, the assistant trainer signed the letter. I remembered him from my visit—a kind-faced man with eyes that sparkled when he talked about sports medicine. The offer included a small stipend to cover my dorm room and some extra cash. It exceeded my expectations.

That evening, I sat on the porch with my Aunt Ella and Uncle Don whom I was living with through my senior year of high school, because of my grandfather's death last year.

"I...I got a letter from the University," I stammered, still in disbelief.

Ella's eyes widened. "Oh, Jimmy! What does it say?"

I handed her the letter, watching as she and Don read it together. Don's face broke into a wide grin. "Well, I'll be damned," he chuckled. "Our boy's going to be a Husker!"

"But," I hesitated, "there's an entrance exam. What if I don't pass?"

Don placed a reassuring hand on my shoulder. "You will, son. You've got more grit than anyone I know. This is your chance—grab it with both hands."

As the weeks flew by, I threw myself into preparation. The day of the exam arrived, and I found myself in Lincoln with Dick Stuckey and Gary Neff. The campus sprawled before us, a maze of red brick and possibility.

"You ready for this, Jim?" Dick asked as we approached the exam building.

I took a deep breath. "As ready as I'll ever be."

The exam was grueling, but as I handed in my paper, a sense of calm washed over me. I had done my best—now it was in fate's hands.

Weeks later, I received confirmation of my acceptance. The realization that I needed $250 for tuition tempered the joy I felt. It seemed an insurmountable sum.

That's when Lyman Stuckey, Dick's father, called me into his bank. Sitting across his imposing desk, I felt small and out of place.

"Jim," he began, speaking with a gruff but kind voice, "I hear you've been accepted to the University."

"Yes, sir," I replied.

"And I also hear you're short on tuition money."

I swallowed hard. "That's right, sir. I'm working to save up, but—"

He held up a hand, silencing me. "I'm going to loan you the $250."

My jaw dropped. "Mr. Stuckey, I...I don't know what to say."

He smiled, a rare sight that transformed his stern face. "Say you'll work hard and make us proud. That's all the thanks I need."

***

As August rolled around, I found myself in a car with Monte Kiffin and Dallas Dyer, heading to Lincoln for fall camp. The closer we got, the more real it all became.

"You nervous, Jimmy?" Monte asked, glancing at me in the rearview mirror.

I nodded, not trusting my voice.

Dallas chuckled from the backseat. "Don't worry, man. We're all in this together. Husker family, right?"

Those words—"Husker family"—echoed in my mind as we pulled into campus. Little did I know how true they would become, or how much that family would come to mean to me in the years ahead.

As we stepped out of the car, the imposing silhouette of Memorial Stadium loomed before us. I took a deep breath, inhaling the scent of cut grass and possibility.

"Well, boys," Monte said, slinging an arm around each of our shoulders, "welcome home."

And just like that, my journey as a member of the Husker family truly began.

Chapter 3: Sweet Opportunities and a New Home

After the first year of attending the university, I had to come back to Lexington for a summer job to earn money for the tuition for my sophomore year. I became employed at Ayers Clothing. After my second week, I entered the store, and the bell's door chimed, cutting through the lazy afternoon activities. I looked up from folding a stack of denim jeans to see a young man I didn't recognize stride in, his eyes scanning the shop before landing on me.

"You, Jim Brown?" he asked, a hint of a smile playing at the corners of his mouth.

Channeling my inner salesman, I straightened up and replied, "Yes, sir. How can I help you today?"

The man's smile widened. "It's more like how I can help you. Name's Bob Sherman. Word on the street is you're heading back to Lincoln for college and could use a job."

My eyebrows shot up in surprise. "That's right. How did you—"

"Small town," Bob chuckled, cutting me off. "Listen, my sister Maryellen works at Russell Stover's candy factory in Lincoln. She's head of HR and might have something for you. Here's her number." He pressed a small piece of paper into my hand.

As I walked Bob out to his delivery truck, the scent of freshly laundered clothes wafting from the back, a surge of hope coursed through me. This could be my ticket to a stable life in Lincoln.

The next morning, with Lyman Stuckey's loan repaid and a mere $50 to my name, I bid farewell to Lexington. Lee Sanks' parting words echoed in my ears as I stepped out onto Highway 30, thumb extended.

"Remember, Jim," he'd said, his eyes twinkling, "sometimes the sweetest opportunities come wrapped in the plainest packages."

The August sun beat down mercilessly as I waited, but luck was on my side. Within minutes, a weather-beaten pickup pulled over.

"Where you headed, son?" the driver called out, his leathery face creased with years of working under the Nebraska sun.

"Lincoln, sir," I replied, hope rising in my chest.

He jerked his thumb toward the passenger seat. "Hop in. I can take you as far as Wood River."

The ride to Wood River flew by in a blur of cornfields and easy conversation. My next ride, a chatty salesman heading to York, regaled me with stories of life on the road.

As I stood on the outskirts of York, the midday sun high overhead, I wondered if I'd made a mistake. Then, like an answer to an unspoken prayer, a massive semi-truck rumbled to a stop beside me.

The driver, a mountain of a man with a beard that would make Santa envious, leaned out of his cab. "Where to, kid?"

"Lincoln," I called back, my voice carrying a mix of hope and desperation.

A booming laugh echoed from the cab. "Well, ain't that a stroke of luck! Climb on up. I'm headed there myself."

As we rolled into Lincoln, the driver, who'd introduced himself as Big Mike, turned to me with a knowing look. "Word of advice, kid. Life's gonna throw you some curves. Just remember, it's not about how hard you can hit, it's about how hard you can get hit and keep moving forward."

With those words ringing in my ears, I found myself on O Street, the heart of downtown Lincoln. The city hummed with an energy I'd never experienced in Lexington, full of possibility and promise.

After a quick call to Maryellen Lorton at Russell Stover's Candy Factory, from a pay phone that smelled faintly of cigarettes and desperation, I made my way to the YMCA. The building loomed before me, a faded brick testament to better days. Maryellen told me I should come to her office tomorrow morning around 8:30 to talk with her about employment.

Inside, the air was thick with the mingled scents of sweat and industrial cleaner. The clerk at the front desk barely looked up as I requested a bed in the dormitory.

"Two weeks'll cost you thirty bucks," he drawled, sliding a key across the scratched counter.

That left me with $20. With my lodging secured and my stomach growling, I ventured out into the sweltering evening. Bishop's Cafeteria beckoned from around the corner, its neon sign a beacon in the gathering twilight. But I didn't dare leave my suitcase in the dormitory, so I brought it with me.

As I sat in the cafeteria, surrounded by the clatter of dishes and the indistinct murmur of conversation, I couldn't help but feel a mix of excitement and trepidation. Tomorrow, I'd meet with Maryellen, and who knew what opportunities awaited?

That night, as I lay on my narrow bed in the YMCA dorm, using my suitcase as a pillow, I stared at the ceiling fan spinning overhead. The room was stifling, the air heavy with heat and the snores of my fellow lodgers. But despite the discomfort, a small smile played on my lips.

"Well, Jim," I whispered to myself, "looks like your Husker journey is just beginning."

***

The next morning, I grabbed my suitcase, got dressed, and began my journey down 10th Street toward the Russell Stover's factory. As I descended the incline, I spotted a restaurant open for breakfast. With only twenty dollars to my name, I decided to stop in for a modest meal. A bowl of oatmeal set me back three dollars, but it would have to suffice.

Continuing down the street, I located the front office and asked for Maryellen, head of hiring, at Russell Stover's. After our interview, she instructed me to return the following day to start work in the jelly department.

On my way back to the YMCA, I revisited the restaurant where I'd had breakfast. I approached the manager with a proposition: having just secured a job at Russell Stover's, could I keep a tab for my daily breakfast and lunch until payday each week? To my relief, he agreed, seeming to sense my trustworthiness. True to my word, I settled my tab that first Friday, and the manager rewarded my honesty with a free lunch. From then on, I enjoyed both breakfast and lunch there on my workdays.

Every afternoon, I'd make my way to the stadium's training room, offering help wherever needed. After a week of renting a locker at the YMCA to safeguard my suitcase, some of the football players began inquiring about my living arrangements for the upcoming semester.

One player, Ron McDole, offered me a solution. He'd found a spare mattress in the Selleck Quad basement and hauled it up to his room, sliding it under his bed. With this opportunity presenting itself, I returned to the YMCA, collected my security deposit, and moved in with Ron.

Ron was an imposing figure—6'4" and around 285 pounds—playing middle linebacker. Hailing from Toledo, Ohio, where he'd played high school ball, Nebraska had recruited him on a scholarship. Little did I know then how this chance arrangement would shape my college experience.

Chapter 4: Summer of Growth

The scorching Nebraska sun beat down on Lexington's main street as I pushed open the door to Ayers Clothing. The bell chimed, announcing my arrival for another day of work. The familiar scent of new leather and starched cotton greeted me, a stark contrast to the locker room smells I'd grown accustomed to at the University.

"Morning, Jim!" John Ayers called from behind the counter, his friendly face creased with a smile. "Ready for another exciting day in the thrilling world of retail?"

I chuckled, hanging up my light jacket. "You bet, Mr. Ayers. Any farmers coming in for work boots today?"

"Now that's the spirit!" Lee Sanks emerged from the stockroom, arms laden with boxes. "Speaking of which, Jim, why don't you restock the shoe display? I've got a feeling we'll have a rush come lunch."

As I arranged the sturdy work boots, my mind wandered to the debt I owed Lyman Stuckey and the upcoming tuition. The weight of responsibility pressed down on me, heavier than any box of shoes.

During a lull in customers, Lee motioned me over to a quiet corner of the store. His eyes, usually twinkling with mischief, were serious. "Jim, sit down a moment. There's something I've been meaning to ask you."

I perched on a nearby stool, curiosity piqued. "What is it, Mr. Sanks?"

He leaned in, his voice gentle. "How did you become an orphan, son?"

The question hit me like a punch to the gut. I'd never spoken about it, not really. But something in Lee's kind eyes made the words tumble out. I told him about my parents, about the orphanage, and living with Grandpa during the summers in Lexington, and the loneliness that had been my constant companion.

As I finished wiping away an errant tear, Lee nodded solemnly. "Jim, thank you for sharing that. You know, I was adopted too."

My eyes widened in surprise. "Really?"

He smiled, a hint of sadness in his eyes. "Oh yes. Only child. But let me give you a piece of advice, Jim. Keep pursuing your dreams. They might change as life throws you curveballs, but never stop chasing them."

That conversation with Lee stayed with me, a beacon of hope in the uncertain seas of my future.

As summer progressed, I found myself drawn into the orbit of Jerry Woodward and Rodney Ranken. Rodney's prized possession was a sleek black Chevy, complete with fender skirts and Smitty mufflers that rumbled like a slumbering beast.

One sweltering evening, Rodney's eyes glinted with mischief. "Boys," he drawled, "how about a little road trip?"

Jerry perked up. "Where to?"

"Phillipsburg, Kansas," Rodney grinned. "It's only sixty miles, and the drinking age is eighteen there."

I hesitated. "I don't know, guys. I'm not much of a drinker."

"Come on, Jimmy," Jerry cajoled. "Live a little!"

Against my better judgment, I found myself squeezed into Rodney's Chevy, the night air whipping through the open windows as we sped toward Kansas. The thrill of rebellion coursed through my veins, momentarily drowning out the voice of reason.

The Chevy's engine roared to life, breaking the quiet of the Lexington night. Rodney grinned as he gunned the engine, the Smitty mufflers rumbling like distant thunder.

"Alright, boys," Rodney called over the noise, "let's make some memories!"

Jerry whooped from the back seat, his excitement palpable. I sat in the passenger seat, a mixture of anticipation and apprehension churning in my stomach.

As we sped down Highway 283, the warm summer air whipping through the open windows, Rodney turned to me with a mischievous glint in his eye.

"Jim, my man, you've got to loosen up. College boy like you should know how to have a good time!"

I forced a smile. "I have good times. They just rarely involve breaking laws."

Jerry leaned forward, clapping me on the shoulder. "Sometimes you gotta bend the rules a little to really live, Jimmy!"

The lights of Phillipsburg appeared on the horizon, a beacon of rebellion in the Kansas night. Rodney pulled into the parking lot of a nondescript liquor store, its neon "OPEN" sign flickering.

"Alright, gents," Rodney announced, "let's get our liquid courage."

Inside, the cool air hit us like a wave. Rodney strode confidently to the counter, slapping down his ID.

"Two cases of Coors, my good man!"

The clerk, a bored-looking man in his fifties, glanced briefly at the ID before nodding toward the cooler. As Rodney and Jerry loaded up, I hung back, suddenly feeling very young and very far from home.

The drive back was a blur of open roads and raucous laughter. Rodney and Jerry took turns swigging from open cans, offering me one every few miles.

"Come on, Jimmy," Jerry cajoled, "just one won't hurt ya!"

Against my better judgment, I accepted. The bitter taste of the beer mixed with the metallic tang of anxiety on my tongue.

By the time we rolled back into Lexington, my head was swimming. The two flights of stairs to my rented room loomed before me like a mountain.

"You good, man?" Rodney called from the car, his words slightly slurred.

I waved him off, concentrating on putting one foot in front of the other.

"Yeah, I'm fine. Thanks for the...adventure."

Each step was a monumental effort, the room tilting and swaying around me. Finally, I tumbled onto my bed, the room spinning like a carnival ride.

Desperately, I remembered a trick I'd overheard some upperclassmen talking about and planted one foot firmly on the floor.

As the spinning slowed, regret washed over me.

"Never again," I muttered to the empty room, my voice sounding small and ashamed. "What would Coach Sullivan think if he could see you now, Jim?"

In the quiet of the night, with the taste of cheap beer still on my tongue, I made a silent promise to myself. I was here to make something of myself, to be part of the Husker family. I couldn't afford to jeopardize that for a few thrills.

As sleep finally claimed me, I resolved to focus on what really mattered—my future at the University and my place in the Husker family. The road trip to Kansas would be my first and last foray into that rebellion.

***

Hours later, as I stumbled up the stairs to my rented room, two flights feeling like twenty, I regretted my decision. Collapsing onto the bed, I placed one foot firmly on the floor, a trick I'd learned to stop the room from spinning. "Never again," I muttered to the empty room.

Little did I know, life had more sobering experiences in store for me. A week later, I received news that my mother had passed away in the State Hospital in Hastings. As I stood before her open casket, memories of the photographs in Grandpa's albums flashed through my mind. Her face was thinner now, but peaceful. In that moment, the weight of my past and the uncertainty of my future collided, leaving me feeling more alone than ever.

The funeral expenses weighed heavily on my mind. Grandpa's children had split the cost four ways among me, Aunt Thelma, Uncle Dwight, and Uncle Don. However, when it came time to settle the bill, Uncle Dwight refused to pay. With a heavy heart but a sense of responsibility, I stepped up and covered his share and my own, using the money I'd earned at Ayers Clothing. It was a financial setback, but I couldn't bear the thought of leaving my mother's final expenses unpaid.

A week after the funeral, an unexpected opportunity arose. Dick Carr, one of my classmates who worked at the funeral parlor, approached me with a proposition.

"Hey Jim," he said, catching me as I was leaving Ayers. "The funeral home owner needs someone to plow a field on his farm. You interested in making some extra cash?"

I nodded eagerly. "Sure, I could use the money. But I've never driven a tractor before."

Dick waved off my concern. "Don't worry, he'll show you the ropes."

That Saturday, I stood in a vast field, the owner's tractor looming before me. The owner gave me a quick tutorial, his words coming fast and assuming some knowledge I didn't possess.

"Keep one front tire against the unturned soil as you go around," he instructed. "When the gas gets low, refuel at the red tank in the yard. Simple enough?"

I nodded, not wanting to appear incompetent. "Got it."

For hours, I circled the field, the monotonous task broken only by trips to refuel. The sun beat down mercilessly and sweat soaked through my shirt. As the day wore on, a sense of accomplishment built. I was doing it!

When the owner returned, I expected praise. Instead, his face fell as he examined the tractor.

The next day, Dick delivered the bad news. "Jim, I'm sorry, but you are the one who burned out the tractor's motor. The boss says you didn't add oil when it was needed."

My heart sank. "Oil? Nobody said anything about oil. I just did what he told me about the gas."

Dick shrugged sympathetically. "Sorry, man. Guess that's what happens when you put a city slicker on a farm job."

I left without a paycheck, the sting of failure sharp and bitter. It was a harsh lesson in the importance of asking questions and not assuming I knew more than I did.

Days later, with bills to pay and a future to secure, I knew I needed to find steady work quickly.

Fortune smiled at me when John Ayers, having heard about my situation through the town grapevine, offered me a position at his clothing store.

"Everyone deserves a second chance, Jim," he'd said, his kind eyes crinkling at the corners. "Besides, we could use a hard worker like you."

Grateful for the opportunity, I threw myself into the job, determined to prove my worth and save enough to return to the University.

After working hard at Ayers Clothing for several weeks, I had finally saved enough to repay Lyman Stuckey's loan. The day I handed him the $250 was bittersweet—a weight lifted off my shoulders, but it left me with only $50 to my name.

As I prepared to leave Lexington, I stopped by the store one last time. Lee Sanks caught me at the door, his eyes twinkling with a mix of pride and concern.

"You've done good work here, Jim," he said, clasping my shoulder. "Remember, sometimes the sweetest opportunities come wrapped in the plainest packages."

With those parting words echoing in my ears and my meager savings in my pocket, I bid farewell to Lexington. The next morning,

I stepped out onto Highway 30, thumb extended, ready to embark on the next chapter of my life.

But fate, it seemed, had other plans. A chance encounter with Bob Sherman at Ayers Clothing led to an unexpected opportunity in Lincoln. As I set out on Highway 30, thumb extended and hope in my heart, I couldn't help but feel that despite the challenges, my Husker dream was still alive.

The journey to Lincoln was an adventure in itself, each ride bringing me closer to my goal. When I finally arrived, the city sprawled before me, a maze of possibilities. With Maryellen number clutched in my hand and Lee Sanks' advice echoing in my mind, I took my first steps toward a new chapter in my life.

That night, as I lay in the stifling YMCA dormitory, my suitcase serving as a pillow, I closed my eyes and dreamed of football fields and futures yet to be written. Tomorrow, I would face Maryellen, HR of Russell Stover's candy factory of Lincoln, Nebraska, along with whatever challenges lay ahead. But for now, surrounded by the snores of strangers, I allowed myself a small smile. The journey was far from over, but I was on my way.

Chapter 5: Conversations from the Jelly Line

As I stood at the end of the massive jelly-making machine at Russell Stover's candy factory, I couldn't help but marvel at the intricate process unfolding before me.

"Hey, new guy!" called out Joe, the head cook. "Ready for another day in sugar paradise?"

I grinned back. "You bet, Joe. Still wrapping my head around all this machinery, though."

Joe chuckled. "Don't worry, son. You'll be dreaming of cornstarch and jellies in no time."

As Joe explained the process, I watched in fascination. The empty wooden trays moved along the conveyor belt, filled with cornstarch and stamped with neat rows of impressions.

"See those little white sacks?" Joe pointed to a stack nearby. "That's where the magic happens."

"What's in them?" I asked, curiosity piqued.

Joe winked. "That's the million-dollar question, kid. Only the big bosses know what's in those top secret ingredient sacks. The formula is specific to Stover's Candies."

As the day wore on, I fell into the rhythm of stacking the heavy trays. My arms ached, but I was determined to keep up.

"You're doing great," encouraged Sarah, one of the veteran workers. "Just remember to lift with your legs, not your back."

"Thanks, Sarah," I puffed, stretching up on my toes to place another tray. "I might need to grow a few inches to reach the top of these stacks!"

Tuesday rolled around, and the starch room ladies joined us. Mary, a cheerful grandmother type, chatted as she placed coconut balls into the jellies.

"You know," she mused, "I've been doing this for fifteen years, and I still get a kick out of seeing how these candies come together."

I nodded, wheeling another tray her way. "It's pretty amazing. But 15 years? That's a long time."

Mary shrugged. "Time flies when you're having fun. Or when you're covered in sugar."

As weeks turned into months, I found myself at the payroll office every Friday. "Here you go, son," said Mr. Thompson, handing me my $50 check. "Another week, another sweet paycheck, eh?"

I forced a smile, but inside, doubts were growing. One day, I approached Joe during our lunch break.

"Joe," I started hesitantly, "how long have you been working here?"

He leaned back, counting on his fingers. "Oh, must be going on thirty years now. Worked my way up from where you are to head cook."

My eyes widened. "Thirty years? And you're just now head cook?"

Joe nodded, as if content. "Yep, that's the way it goes. Why? Are you planning your rise to the top already?"

I chuckled nervously. "Just thinking about the future."

That night, as I looked at my meager savings, I made a decision. The next morning, I approached my supervisor.

"Mr. Johnson," I said, "I've been thinking. I'd like to reduce my hours. I want to go back to school."

He looked surprised. "School? But you've got a steady job here. Why would you want to leave?"

I took a deep breath. "I appreciate everything I've learned here, but I think there might be more opportunities out there for me with more education."

Mr. Johnson nodded slowly. "Well, I can't say I'm not disappointed to lose a good worker, but I understand. Education is important. We'll work out a schedule for you."

As I left his office, I felt a mix of excitement and nervousness. The jelly department had been my world for six months, but now it was time for a new chapter. Who knew? Maybe one day I'd return to Russell Stover's—but next time, it might be in a suit and tie, running the entire operation.

Chapter 6: A Greyhound Adventure to Baseball's Spring Training

I settled into a chair in the university's treatment room, facing George Sullivan, our trusted athletic trainer. "Hey George," I started, curiosity getting the better of me, "what's the deal with trainers for major league baseball teams? Seems like it could be an interesting gig."

George leaned back, a thoughtful look on his face. "Well, from what I've heard at conventions, they've got it pretty easy for injuries. Why do you ask?"

"I might want to look into it," I replied, my mind already racing with possibilities.

George's eyes lit up. "You know what? Most baseball teams have their spring camps down in Florida. That's where you should go if you want information. Who knows? You might even snag a job while you're at it!"

Taking George's advice to heart, I marched into Maryellen's office at Russell Stover's.

"Maryellen," I began, sounding confident, "could I take three weeks off? I'm planning a trip to Florida to talk with some baseball trainers."

Maryellen looked at me for a moment, then smiled. "Alright, but make sure you come back to us when you're done chasing your baseball dreams."

With her blessing, I headed to the Greyhound depot, ticket to Tampa in hand and a letter of recommendation from George tucked securely in my pocket. As I boarded the bus, little did I know I was in for a three-day, four-night journey that would open my eyes to a world beyond Nebraska.

Somewhere in Alabama, an elderly gentleman in a crisp white suit sat next to me. "First time down South, son?" he drawled.

"Yes, sir," I replied, taking in the unfamiliar landscape outside the window.

He leaned in closer, his voice low. "Well, let me tell you about how things work down here with the Negroes..."

I listened, shocked and confused. This was a far cry from my experiences with Thunder Thornton and Clay White, some of the first Black football players in Nebraska.

Days later, as we approached Tampa, the kind-hearted bus driver turned to me. "Where you headed, kid?"

"I'm not sure," I admitted. "I'm looking for baseball spring training camps."

He chuckled. "You want Clearwater, not Tampa. Tell you what, why don't you catch some shut-eye in the back of the bus? I'll have the gatekeeper wake you in the morning."

True to his word, I was awakened by a banging on the bus side. The depot gatekeeper grinned as he opened the door. "Welcome to Tampa, Jim! Hope you slept well."

After a quick call to my Uncle Frank in Clearwater, I found myself on yet another bus. As we pulled into Clearwater, I spotted my elderly uncle and his wife Ethel waving enthusiastically.

"Jimmy!" Uncle Frank called out, pulling me into a hug. "My, how you've grown!"

Over lunch, I regaled them with tales of my journey. "You wouldn't believe the things I saw and heard, Uncle Frank. It's like a whole different world down here."

Uncle Frank nodded sagely. "Oh, I believe it. Things are changing, but slowly. Now, tell me more about this baseball trainer idea of yours."

As we chatted, I couldn't help but feel a mix of excitement and nervousness. Here I was, far from home, pursuing a dream I scarcely understood. But with my family's support and George's letter in my pocket, I felt ready to take on whatever challenges lay ahead in the world of baseball.

Chapter 7: From Dugouts to Hotel Management

I settled into Uncle Frank and Aunt Ethel's cozy Clearwater home, which became my temporary baseball headquarters for three exciting weeks. Aunt Ethel, a fountain of local knowledge, spent hours helping me track down addresses for the spring training camps and explaining the intricacies of the local bus system.

One morning, as we sat at the kitchen table, Aunt Ethel spread out a hand-drawn map. "Now Jimmy," she said, her fingers tracing the routes, "the bus stop is just two blocks down on Maple Street. That'll get you to all the ballparks. But remember, timing is everything with these buses."

Uncle Frank chimed in from behind his newspaper, "And don't forget to take some water with you. Florida sun can be mighty unforgiving."

Armed with their advice and barely contained excitement, I set out for my first stop: the Philadelphia Phillies at Jack Russell Stadium. As I entered the clubhouse, the smell of leather and liniment hit me, and I felt like a kid in a candy store. Players milled about, their chatter filling the air. I approached a player sitting by his locker, the nameplate reading 'Joe Coker'.

"Excuse me," I said, keeping my voice steady, "could you point me to the training room?"

Joe looked up from lacing his cleats and smiled. "Sure, kid. Head down to the end of the lockers and turn left. Can't miss it. Ask for Bob when you get there."

"Thanks, Mr. Coker," I replied, then added nervously, "Good luck this season."

He chuckled, "Thanks, kid. We'll need it."

I found Bob the trainer in the training room, taping a player's ankle with practiced ease. "Hi there," I said, handing him George Sullivan's letter. "I'm a student trainer from the University of Nebraska. I was wondering if you might need any help?"

Bob read the letter, then looked at me with a mix of amusement and sympathy. "Sorry, kid. We usually hire from within the organization. It's just how things work here. But tell you what, stick around today, see how we operate. Might learn a thing or two."

I spent the day observing, soaking in every detail from how they taped ankles to the way they handled more serious injuries. As I waited for my bus back, I watched batting practice, marveling at the skill of pitcher Ruben Gomez.

That evening, over dinner with Uncle Frank and Aunt Ethel, I regaled them with tales of my day. "You should've seen Gomez pitch, Uncle Frank! And the training room, it's like a mini hospital!"

The next day, fueled by my experience with the Phillies, I set my sights on the New York Yankees at Al Lang Stadium. As I entered the locker room, I found myself face-to-face with baseball royalty.

"Excuse me," I stammered, my eyes wide as saucers, "I'm looking for the training room."

Yogi Berra, sitting on a bench tying his shoes, looked up at me. "Down at the end, turn right. Trainer's name is Jack Moncato." Then he added with a grin, "And remember, kid, it ain't over 'til it's over."

I thanked him, still in awe that I'd just spoken to Yogi Berra, and made my way to the training room.

Jack Moncato was friendly, but didn't have any openings. He did, however, mention a clubhouse manager position opening up in Tri-Cities.

"It's where I started fourteen years ago," he explained, leaning against the treatment table. "You'd manage travel arrangements, meals, laundry, and help with injuries. Pays about $300 a month to start."

"What's the career path like?" I asked, imagining my future.

Jack scratched his chin. "Well, if you work hard, you could move up to a Double-A team in a few years, then Triple-A. It might take fifteen to twenty years to make it to the majors as a trainer, but it's possible."

I left with Jack's card, but the more I thought about it on the bus ride home, the more I realized this wasn't the path for me. I wanted more than to spend years working my way up to maybe, someday, become a major league trainer.

Back at Uncle Frank's, I scoured the local papers. An ad for hotel management classes in Tampa caught my eye. It promised a quicker path to a stable career, and suddenly, a new possibility opened up before me.

"Uncle Frank," I said over our nightly gin rummy game, my cards forgotten in my hand, "I'm going to give this hotel management course a try."

He laid down his cards and looked at me over his glasses. "Hotel management, eh? That's quite a change from baseball, Jimmy."

"I know," I replied, "but it might be a better fit for me. More opportunities, you know?"

He nodded approvingly. "Good thinking, Jimmy. It's important to keep your options open. Here's $300 to get you started. Consider it an investment in your future."

With Aunt Ethel's help, I navigated the bus system to Tampa, registered for classes, and found a boarding house. The lady who ran it, Mrs. Peterson, reminded me of Aunt Ethel with her kind smile and no-nonsense attitude.

"Dinner's at 6:00 p.m. sharp," she told me as she showed me to my room. "Don't be late, or you'll go hungry."

As I settled into my new routine, I called Aunt Ethel to update her.

"I'm all set up, Aunt Ethel. Classes start Monday. The boarding house is nice, and Mrs. Peterson seems great."

"That's wonderful, dear," she replied, the warmth in her voice carrying over the line. "Just remember to keep in touch. We worry about you, you know. And don't forget to eat your vegetables!"

As I hung up, I couldn't help but feel a mix of excitement and nervousness. My baseball dreams might be on hold, but a new adventure was just beginning. The first day of class, I sat in the front row, notebook open, ready to learn.

"Welcome to Hotel Management 101," the instructor began. "By the end of this course, you'll know everything from front desk operations to housekeeping logistics."

As I jotted down notes, I thought to myself, "Who knew? Maybe one day I'll be managing a hotel where baseball teams stay during spring training."

The idea made me smile. Life has a funny way of coming full circle sometimes.

Chapter 8: A Small-Town Boy's Eye-Opening Experience

As I settled into my routine at the hotel management school in Tampa, I found myself in a peculiar situation. Despite being surrounded by classmates, I struggled to form close relationships. Most of my peers either lived with their parents or worked night jobs, leaving little room for socializing. To combat the loneliness, I developed a nightly ritual: after dinner, I'd make my way to a local coffeehouse, losing myself in the melodies of local musicians until fatigue sent me back to my boarding house.

One balmy Florida evening, as I sat alone at my usual table in the crowded coffeehouse, a young man about my age approached. With a smile, he gestured to the empty chair across from me.

"Mind if I join you? Seems like every other seat in the house is taken," he said, his voice warm and friendly.

I nodded, welcoming the company. As we chatted, I learned his name was Alex. He had an easygoing manner that put me at ease, and soon we were laughing and swapping stories as if we'd known each other for years.

As the night wore on, Alex leaned in and asked, "Do you like to party?"

My small-town Nebraska upbringing hadn't prepared me for much partying, but I didn't want to seem boring.

"Sure, I love to party," I replied with more enthusiasm than experience.

Alex's eyes lit up. "Great! I've got a bunch of friends throwing a shindig this weekend. Why don't you come along? I can pick you up around noon on Sunday."

Excited at the prospect of making new friends, I agreed and gave him my address. As Sunday rolled around, I stood on the walkway outside my boarding house, a mix of anticipation and nervousness fluttering in my stomach.

Right on time, Alex pulled up in a beat-up Chevy. As we drove, he kept up a steady stream of chatter, telling me about his friends and the party. I nodded, trying to quell the butterflies in my stomach.

When we arrived, I was surprised the house was completely devoid of furniture. About twenty guys milled about, lounging on the floor with drinks in hand. What struck me most was the absence of any girls. Still, I brushed it off, figuring they might show up later.

Alex, ever the gracious host, got me a drink—a C&C, my go-to at the time—and introduced me to some of his friends. The atmosphere was lively, with excited chatter about Johnny Mathis supposedly making an appearance later.

As I sipped my drink, I couldn't help but notice the way the guys interacted with each other. There was an intimacy to their gestures, a softness in their voices that I wasn't accustomed to seeing between men. Still, I chalked it up to close friendships and continued to enjoy my drink.

After my second C&C, a wave of dizziness washed over me. I closed my eyes, steadying myself. When I opened them again, I found Alex lying on the floor in front of me, his elbows propped against my crossed legs, chin cupped in his hands. He was staring at me with an intensity that made me uncomfortable.

"You okay?" he asked, his voice laced with concern. "Maybe we should go somewhere quieter. How about the back bedroom?"

In that moment, realization hit me like a ton of bricks. The absence of girls, the intimate gestures, Alex's intense gaze—it all clicked into place. These weren't just close friends; they were gay men. Growing up in small-town Nebraska, I had never knowingly encountered anyone who was gay. Now, here I was, in a house full of gay men, with one making what I perceived as advances toward me.

Panic rose in my chest. "I...I want to go home," I stammered, my discomfort evident in my voice. "I don't feel comfortable here."

Alex's face fell, a mix of disappointment and understanding crossing his features. "Are you sure? We could just talk..."

"Please," I insisted, "take me home."

To his credit, Alex didn't push the issue. He helped me to my feet and led me out to his car. As we drove back to my boarding house, an awkward silence hung between us.

Finally, Alex spoke. "I'm sorry you feel this way. I can understand your position, though. I should have been more upfront about the nature of the party."

I nodded, unsure of what to say. My mind was reeling, processing this new experience. I felt a confusing mix of emotions—shock at my naivety, embarrassment at my reaction, and a twinge of guilt for hurting Alex's feelings.

As we pulled up to my boarding house, Alex turned to me. "Look, I hope this doesn't color your view of all of us. We're just people, finding our place in the world, same as you."

His words stuck with me long after I'd gone inside. As I lay in bed that night, I couldn't help but reflect on the evening's events. I realized that my reaction had been born out of surprise and unfamiliarity rather than any real prejudice. Still, I felt out of my depth in Tampa, like I was playing a game where everyone else knew the rules but me.

The next morning, I took stock of my situation. My funds were running low, with only two weeks of classes left before graduation from the hotel management program. The thought of asking Uncle Frank for more money made me cringe. Despite the valuable skills I'd learned, I couldn't shake the feeling that I was adrift, far from the familiar comforts of home.

With a heavy heart, I made my decision. I said goodbye to the school and the boarding house, then used my last bit of change to call Uncle Frank from a payphone.

"Uncle Frank?" I said when he picked up. "I'm coming home. I think...it's time for me to try getting back into college in Nebraska."

As I hung up the phone, I felt a mix of relief and disappointment. Tampa had been an eye-opening experience in more ways than one, but it had also shown me how much growing I still had to do. As I boarded the bus back to Nebraska, I couldn't help but wonder what other surprises life had in store for me. One thing was certain—my worldview had expanded, and there was no going back to the naïve small-town boy I'd been when I first arrived in Florida.

Chapter 9: Boxing, Dorm Life, and Candy Factory Chronicles

As the Greyhound bus rolled into Lincoln, I felt a mix of relief and anticipation. The familiar landscape of Nebraska welcomed me back, and I couldn't help but smile. I was home, ready to tackle another semester at the university and resume my job at Russell Stover's.

The next morning, I made my way to the candy factory. Maryellen, my supervisor, greeted me with a warm smile. "Welcome back, Jim! Ready to jump back into the jelly department?"

"You bet, Maryellen," I replied, tying on my apron. "It's good to be back."

The rhythmic hum of machinery and the sweet scent of sugar enveloped me as I settled into my old routine. Summer classes occupied my mornings, while afternoons and evenings were spent at the factory, trying to earn enough for the upcoming semester's tuition.

A few weeks into the semester, I ran into Ron McDole in the dorm hallway. "Hey, Jimmy!" he called out. "How's the living situation treating you?"

I shrugged. "It's alright. The locker room's not ideal, but it works for now."

Ron's face lit up. "I've got an idea. Why don't you move in with me and Pete Peterson? We've got some floor space."

His offer was a godsend, and I gratefully accepted. However, my living arrangements were about to change again. One evening, as I was heading to Ron's room, Dallas, and Mick Tinglehoff cornered me in the hallway.

"Jimmy, we need to talk," Dallas said, a mischievous glint in his eye.

Mick nodded, adding, "We've got a proposition for you."

Intrigued, I followed them to their room. There, taking up a good portion of the small space, was a well-worn wicker couch.

"Ta-da!" Dallas exclaimed, gesturing grandly. "Your new bed, if you want it."

Mick chimed in, "Yeah, we figured you'd be more comfortable here than on Ron's floor. Plus, we can bring you dinner from the training table every evening."

Their generosity touched me. "Are you guys sure? I don't want to impose."

"Impose? Nah," Mick laughed. "Consider it rent for all the contraband you bring us from the candy factory."

I felt my face flush. "You know about that?"

Dallas clapped me on the shoulder. "Jimmy, the whole dorm knows about your nut room raids. Speaking of which..."

I grinned, reaching into my pockets to produce handfuls of pecans, almonds, and cashews. "Special delivery, gentlemen."

Our little arrangement worked well. I'd return from Russell Stover's around 5:30 each evening, pockets bulging with nuts or chunks of chocolate, to find a hot meal waiting for me. The guys would regale me with tales from football practice as we ate.

One evening, as we were finishing dinner, I shared a story from work. "You wouldn't believe what happened today. I was helping break up these massive Hershey's chocolate blocks—we're talking 150 pounds each."

"No way," Dallas said, his eyes wide. "How do you even move something like that?"

I demonstrated the technique. "You grab one end, lift it as high as you can, then let it drop. The impact breaks it into smaller pieces. Ralph then picks up the broken pieces and places them through a hole in the floor into these two giant melting vats that are in the basement. The chocolate is piped up to the third floor where the pipes are wrapped with electric-heated wires. There are two different pipes: one for dark chocolate and another for light chocolate.

Mick whistled. "Sounds like quite an operation. You ever think about how many candy bars that makes?"

I shook my head, laughing. "Trust me, after a day in the factory, the last thing I want to think about is more candy."

Life settled into a comfortable routine until George Haney burst into our room one afternoon, his face flushed with excitement. "Jimmy! There you are. I've been looking all over for you."

I looked up from my book, confused. "What's up, George?"

He grabbed a chair, spinning it around to sit backwards, facing me. "You need to get into the Golden Gloves boxing club. There's a regional tournament coming up in Lincoln."

I felt my stomach drop. "Boxing? George, I don't know. I've only had one fight in high school, and it wasn't pretty."

George waved off my concerns. "Steve Smith told me you fought for his dad at the National Guard summer camp. Come on, I'll be your trainer. I'll whip you into shape!"

Despite my reservations, George's enthusiasm was infectious. Before I knew it, I found myself in the field house weight room the next day, facing a hanging punching bag.

George handed me a pair of light leather gloves with one-pound weights across the palms. "Alright, Jimmy. I want you to hit this bag for thirty seconds, rest for forty-five, then go again. Keep going until I tell you to stop."

As I pounded the bag, George continued, "We've got two weeks before fight night. Meet me here every day. And I want you running three laps around the track daily—that's a mile. I'll time you to make sure you're improving your breathing."

The next two weeks were a blur of training sessions, runs, and work at Russell Stover's. My arms ached, my lungs burned, but I was determined to give it my all.

Back in the dorm, Dallas and Mick got in on the action, helping me train with light sparring sessions after dinner. It was all fun and games until Dallas upped the ante.

"Jim," he said one evening, a serious look on his face. "We may need to spar for real. Full strength. You need to be ready for the actual fight."

I hesitated. "I don't know, Dallas. I don't want to hurt you."

He scoffed. "Hurt me? Come on, give it your best shot."

Reluctantly, I took a fighting stance. I threw a quick left jab, which Dallas easily blocked with his right forearm. Feeling a bit more confident, I followed up with a right hook. To both our surprises, it connected solidly with his left eye.

Dallas let out a yelp of pain, his hand flying to his face. "Oh my God," I stammered. "Dallas, I'm so sorry. I didn't mean to hit you that hard."

His face had turned an alarming shade of red, but he managed a pained smile. "See? I didn't expect that right. Good job."

I rushed to the bathroom, returning with a cold washcloth. "Here, put this on it. It doesn't look too bad, just a red mark above your eye."

The next day, Dallas sported a pair of sunglasses to hide his impressive shiner. This didn't deter Mick from volunteering as my sparring partner the next day.

"Alright, Brownie," Mick said, using my nickname. "Let's go. I'll only use one arm, but you have to hit me with all you've got."

I was even more hesitant after the incident with Dallas. "I don't know, Mick. You're a lot bigger than me. I don't want to risk hurting you."

Mick laughed. "Hurt me? Come on, I'm a football player. I can take it. Now get your hands up."

Reluctantly, I raised my fists. Mick, true to his word, only had his left arm up. I threw a tentative jab, connecting with his left eye. Mick stood there, looking surprised for a moment.

Then, without warning, he pressed his left arm against my chest, pushed me back, and followed up with a powerful left to my sternum. The force of the blow lifted me off my feet, sending me flying across the room. I crashed into the wall, feeling the drywall give way behind me.

As I sat there, gasping for breath, surrounded by broken drywall, Mick started laughing. "See? I didn't even need my other arm."

The night of the tournament arrived all too quickly. George picked me up, armed with gauze, boxing shoes, and gloves. As we drove to the Lincoln auditorium, I felt a mix of excitement and terror.

In the dressing room, George carefully wrapped my hands, his movements precise and practiced. "Remember," he said as he worked, "keep throwing your left, walk to your left around the ring. When you see his right hand come, step right and throw your right at his body."

As we approached the ring, I heard the announcer's voice boom through the speakers: "In the red corner, weighing in at 135 pounds, with a record of fourteen fights and ten wins, please welcome Mike 'The Hammer' Johnson!"

The crowd cheered as my opponent raised his gloved hands. Then, the announcer continued, "And in the blue corner, weighing in at 132 pounds, with a record of 2 fights and no wins, Jim Brown!"

The polite applause that followed did little to boost my confidence. As I climbed into the ring, George gave me a reassuring pat on the back. "You've got this, Jimmy. Remember what we practiced."

The bell rang, and suddenly, I was face to face with 'The Hammer.' I circled left, just as George had taught me, throwing jabs when I saw an opening. To my surprise, I landed a few solid body shots, causing my opponent to step back.

"That's it, Jimmy!" I heard George shout from my corner. "Keep going at it!"

Encouraged, I pressed forward, throwing combinations of rights and lefts until the bell rang, signaling the end of the first round. I collapsed onto the small stool in my corner, gulping air.

George was there immediately, squirting water into my mouth and pouring the rest over my head. "You're doing great, kid," he said. "Now, keep those left jabs coming, aim for his jaw. When he steps back, that's your chance to bring up that right to his chin."

The second round was tougher. My arms felt heavier, and 'The Hammer' seemed to have found his rhythm. I took several hard shots to the face, but stayed on my feet until the bell rang.

By the third round, I was running on fumes. My legs felt like lead, and it was all I could do to keep my hands up. The final bell was a relief, even though I knew I hadn't won.

As the referee raised my opponent's hand in victory, George helped me out of the ring. "You did good, Jimmy," he said, his voice full of pride. "Real good."

The next morning, still sore from the fight, I dragged myself to work at Russell Stover's. To my surprise, my supervisor approached me mid-shift. "Jim, the president wants to see you in the main office."

Nervously, I made my way to Maryellen's office. She smiled reassuringly as she led me to the president's door. "Don't worry," she whispered. "It's nothing bad."

The president, a distinguished-looking man in his sixties, gestured for me to take a seat. "Jim," he began, "how's school going?"

"It's going well, sir," I replied, hiding my nervousness. "I've saved enough for next semester's classes."

He nodded approvingly. "Good, good. You know, Jim, you remind me of Little Lord Fauntleroy. Always coming and going, but never failing to work hard when you're here. The supervisors speak highly of you."

I felt a warmth spread through my chest at his words. "Thank you, sir. I really appreciate the opportunity to work here."

He leaned forward, his expression serious. "I want you to know that we're here to help you through college, Jim. If you ever need anything—extra hours, time off for exams, anything at all—my door is always open."

As I left his office, I felt a renewed sense of determination. With the support of Russell Stover's, my friends in the dorm, and my own hard work, I knew I could make it through college.

The rest of the semester flew by. As a PE major, I shared many classes with the football players, which turned out to be a blessing in disguise. Larry Kramer, Lloyd Voss, and Mick would often pick up extra textbooks for me when getting their free ones.

"Here you go, Jimmy," Larry would say, handing me a stack of books. "Just make sure you return them at the end of the semester so we can turn them back in."

Their generosity saved me a significant expense, allowing me to stretch my Russell Stover's paycheck even further.

As Thanksgiving approached, Ron McDole surprised me with an unexpected offer. "Hey, Jimmy," he said one evening, "I've got an extra plane ticket to Toledo for Thanksgiving. Want to come home with me?"

I was taken aback by his generosity. "Are you serious, Ron? That's...that's incredibly kind of you."

He grinned. "Consider it payback for all those late-night study sessions. Besides, it'll be fun to show you around my hometown."

After getting the okay from Russell Stover's for a two-week break, I found myself on a plane to Ohio. Toledo was a whirlwind of new experiences. Ron introduced me to his family, his high school friends, and his high school sweetheart, Paula.

"Paula's a hell of a swimmer," Ron told me proudly. "She's on the University of Ohio team now."

Paula, a strong, athletic girl with a warm smile, hit it off with me immediately. "So you're the famous Jimmy," she said, her eyes twinkling. "Ron's told me all about your adventures in the dorm."

The visit flew by, filled with family dinners, tours of Ron's old haunts, and even a chance to watch Paula at swim practice. And just like that, it was time to return to Lincoln.

As we squeezed into Ron's tiny Fiat for the drive back, I couldn't help but reflect on how much my world had expanded since coming to the university. From the jelly department at Russell Stover's to the boxing ring, from dorm room hijinks to out-of-state adventures, I was experiencing life in ways I never imagined back in my small Nebraska town.

Settling back into my routine at the candy factory, I was promoted to the Turtle department. After the holidays, I felt a renewed sense of purpose. Sure, the work was hard and balancing it with classes was a constant challenge. But with each paycheck, each passing grade, and each new friendship, I was building a future for myself.

As I stood at my station in the Turtle department, watching the endless parade of candy trays filled with pecans, nuts, and special caramel nuggets, I smiled to myself. Life was sweet, in more ways than one, and I was determined to savor every moment.

Chapter 10: Home with Archie and Annette

The spring semester was in full swing, and I was finally finding my rhythm. As I walked out of my last class for the day, I spotted Archie and Annette waving at me from across the quad. Archie was the kicker for the team. He and George Haney were the transferred older players from Georgia Tech who were best of friends.

"Hey there!" Archie called out, his tall frame easily visible over the crowd. "How's it going?"

I jogged over to them, adjusting my backpack. "Pretty good, actually. I've finally gotten my schedule sorted out."

Annette's eyes lit up with interest. "Oh? How so?"

"Well," I began, falling into step beside them, "I've arranged my classes around my shifts at Russell Stover's. It's been a juggling act, but I've got it down now."

Archie whistled, impressed. "That's no small feat. How're you liking the job?"

I grinned, "It's sweet...literally! But seriously, it's not bad. Helps pay the bills, you know?"

As we walked toward the student center, Annette suddenly turned to me with an excited expression. "Say, we've been meaning to ask you something."

"Oh?" I raised an eyebrow, curious.

Archie nodded, a warm smile on his face. "Yeah, would you like to join us for the Easter break? We're heading down to Mobile, Alabama—that's where I grew up."

I blinked in surprise. "Really? You want me to come along?"

Annette laughed, linking her arm through mine. "Of course we do! It'll be fun to have you along. Plus, you could use a break from all this studying and working."

The offer was tempting. I had made no plans for the break, and the idea of getting away from campus for a while was appealing.

"Are you sure I wouldn't be intruding?"

Archie clapped a hand on my shoulder. "Not at all. My folks always love having guests, and there's plenty of room. What do you say?"

A grin spread across my face. "Well, in that case, I'd love to come! Thanks, guys."

The next couple of weeks flew by in a flurry of exams and work shifts. Before I knew it, I was tossing my duffel bag into the trunk of Archie's car, ready for our road trip to Mobile.

Archie took the wheel, with Annette riding shotgun and I sprawled out in the back seat. As we pulled away from campus, Annette turned to me with a mischievous glint in her eye.

"So, ready for fourteen hours of quality time with us?"

I laughed, settling back into my seat. "Bring it on!"

The drive was long, but far from boring. We swapped stories, sang along (badly) to the radio, and played endless rounds of I Spy. Archie regaled us with tales from his childhood in Mobile, painting a vivid picture of the town I was about to visit.

"You'll love it," he assured me as we crossed the Alabama state line. "It's got a charm all its own."

Despite the lengthy journey, Archie seemed tireless behind the wheel. As the sun rose, painting the sky in soft pinks and golds, we finally pulled into a quiet neighborhood in Mobile.

"Home sweet home," Archie announced, parking in front of a charming two-story house with a wide front porch.

As we stumbled out of the car, stretching our cramped limbs, the front door swung open. A woman who could only be Archie's mother stepped out, a warm smile on her face.

"Welcome home, honey!" she called out. "Y'all must be exhausted. Are you hungry? How about some breakfast?"

Archie grinned, giving his mother a big hug. "Mom, you're the best. Oh, this is my friend from school," he said, gesturing toward me.

I stepped forward, suddenly feeling shy. "It's nice to meet you, Mrs. Cobb. Thank you for having me."

"Oh, nonsense," she waved off my thanks. "Any friend of Archie's is welcome here. Now come on in, all of you. Ruthie's been up since dawn, cooking up a storm."

As we entered the house, the smell of coffee and something deliciously sweet wafted through the air. Following Mrs. Cobb into the kitchen, I was introduced to Ruthie, a kind-faced black woman who had clearly been waiting eagerly for our arrival.

"Oh, Archie!" she exclaimed, pulling him into a tight hug. "Let me look at you, child! Have you been eating enough?"

Archie laughed, returning the hug with equal enthusiasm. "Ruthie's been with us for twenty-two years," he explained to me. "She practically raised me."

"And don't you forget it," Ruthie chuckled, already bustling back to the stove. "Now, who wants some of Archie's favorite cinnamon toast?"

As we sat down at the kitchen table, I couldn't help but feel a warmth that had nothing to do with the steaming plates of food being set before us. There was a sense of home here, of belonging, that was palpable.

Ruthie outdid herself with breakfast. Fried eggs, grits (my first time trying them), and the promised cinnamon toast were all laid out before us. Archie and I, ravenous after the long drive, dug in with gusto.

"Lord have mercy," Ruthie exclaimed, shaking her head in amusement as she watched us polish off over a dozen eggs between the two of us. "You boys sure can eat!"

The next few days passed in a whirlwind of activity. Archie took me on a tour of Mobile, showing me his old haunts and introducing me to what felt like half the town. Everyone seemed to know him, and by extension, welcomed me with open arms.

One afternoon, as we were driving back from meeting some of Archie's high school football buddies, I decided to satisfy my curiosity about something.

"Hey Archie," I began, "I didn't know you played anything other than kicker in college."

Archie chuckled, his eyes on the road. "Yeah, well, it's a bit of a story. You know, I almost went to Georgia Tech."

"Really?" I leaned forward, intrigued. "What happened?"

He sighed, a rueful smile on his face. "Well, Bernie Haney—you've met him in Nebraska, right?—and I both got recruited to Georgia Tech. But we, uh, got into a bit of trouble there."

"Trouble?" I prompted when he fell silent.

Archie nodded, his expression a mix of embarrassment and amusement. "Let's just say we made some poor choices at a party. Nothing too serious, but enough that we decided it was best to transfer. We both ended up at Nebraska on football scholarships."

I whistled low. "Wow, I had no idea. So how did you end up as a kicker?"

"Well," Archie began, chuckling, "at 6'5" and 220 pounds, they naturally tried to make me a lineman. But here's the thing—I wasn't too fond of getting hit. Like, at all."

I couldn't help but laugh at this. Archie, with his imposing frame, seemed like he'd be a natural on the line.

"I know, I know," he grinned, seeing my reaction. "But one day during practice, we were messing around during a water break, and I kicked the ball. Turns out, I had a pretty good leg. The coach saw it, and well, the rest is history."

As the week drew to a close, I felt surprisingly at home in Mobile. Archie's family and friends had welcomed me with open arms, and I'd experienced a slice of Southern hospitality that I'd only ever heard about.

On our last night, as we sat on the front porch watching the sunset, Annette turned to me. "So, what did you think of your Alabama adventure?"

I smiled, taking in the peaceful scene before me. "It's been amazing. Thank you both for inviting me. I...I feel like I've found a second home here."

Archie nodded, a knowing look in his eyes. "That's Mobile for you. It has a way of getting under your skin."

As we packed up the car the next morning, ready for the long drive back to Nebraska, I already looked forward to the next time I could visit. This Easter break had given me more than just a vacation. It had given me a new perspective, new friends, and memories I knew I'd cherish for years to come.

Chapter 11: Summer Workout at the Field House

The Nebraska summer sun was beating down something fierce as I wiped the sweat from my brow. I was standing outside the field house, waiting for Mac Dole to pull up in his new ride.

"Hey there, buddy!" Mac called out as he rolled up in a tiny Fiat. "Hop in! What do you think of my new wheels?"

I couldn't help but chuckle as I squeezed into the passenger seat. "Well, I'll be. It's sure is...compact. But hey, at least we won't have to hoof it around town anymore."

Mac grinned, patting the dashboard affectionately. "That's the spirit! Now, let's go pick up Clay. We have a long day ahead of us."

As we cruised through the quiet streets of Lincoln, I turned to Mac. "So, how'd you and Clay land this construction gig?"

"Oh, you know how it is," Mac replied, navigating a turn. "The coaches pulled some strings. Got us set up with the highway department for the summer. They're working on a few bridges which cross over the I-80 between here and Omaha."

We pulled up to the curb where Clay White was waiting, looking none too thrilled about the early hour.

"Rise and shine, fellas!" I called out, earning a couple of groggy glares in return.

Clay yawned as he crammed himself into the back seat. "Easy for you to say. You ain't the one who's gotta be on site at 6:00 a.m. sharp."

Clay nodded in agreement.

Ron then turned toward me stating, "Yeah, and you, Brownie, get to head back to your cushy job at Russell Stover's."

I held up my hands in mock surrender. "Hey now, don't be jealous. Someone's gotta make sure them chocolates get made."

The drive to the construction site was filled with good-natured ribbing and talk about the upcoming football season. As I dropped the guys off, Ron leaned in through the window.

"Don't forget, you have to be here at 5:30 to pick us up because we're meeting at the field house after work for training. You're joining us, right?"

I nodded, "Wouldn't miss it for the world. Now get to work, you slackers!"

As I drove back to Lincoln, I couldn't help but feel a twinge of sympathy for the guys. The dorms were closed for the summer, and the athletic department's solution was less than ideal.

Later that afternoon, after I got off from working at Russell Stover's, I drove McDole's Fiat out to the bridge to pick up Ron and Clay after they got off work. We three walked into the field house to find a sea of mattresses spread out on the floor. A couple players were sprawled out on some of the mattresses, looking beat.

"Rough day?" I asked, plopping down next to one of them.

Larry Cramer groaned, throwing an arm over his eyes. "You have no idea. But hey, at least we've got a roof over our heads and showers. Some of the other boys are bunking with local families or working for the night shift on the police department."

Just then, Archie Cobb burst in, looking far too energetic for someone who'd just finished a day's work. "Alright, ladies! Time to shake off the dust and hit the track. We've got a season to prepare for!"

There was a chorus of groans, but slowly, everyone got up. We made our way out to the stadium; the cinder track a dull red in the late afternoon light.

Archie clapped a hand on my shoulder. "How about it? Fancy a run around the track?"

I shrugged. "Sure, why not? Don't you want to start with running the stadium stairs first? There are only 100 steps up, and another 100 down, or do you want me to take a lap, and you fellas can keep up?"

Ron snorted. "Big talk for a chocolate maker. Let's see what you've got. Stairs are for a running back not a lineman as of yet."

And so began our summer routine. I'd take off around the track, with Ron and Archie huffing and puffing behind me. At first, they could barely make it halfway around before collapsing in a sweaty heap.

"Lord have mercy." Ron wheezed after one particularly grueling session. We had worked up to three laps after a week of practice. "I thought I was in shape, but this is something else."

Archie nodded, bent over with his hands on his knees. "Yeah, but we're getting better. Mark my words, by the end of summer, we'll be running circles around you."

I grinned, hardly winded. "I'll believe it when I see it, boys."

As the weeks wore on, true to Archie's word, they improved. By August, they were jogging the full mile without too much trouble.

One evening, after our run, Archie grabbed a football. "Hey, how about some punting practice?"

I shrugged, "Sure, why not?"

Archie jogged down to the far end of the field, while I stayed at the other end to catch his punts. He started punting, each kick soaring high into the air.

"Looking good, Arch!" I called out, snagging another punt.

He grinned, setting up for another kick. "Just you wait, I'm gonna really let this one fly!"

True to his word, the next punt went stratospheric. I lost sight of it against the setting sun, squinting to spot it.

"Uh oh," I muttered, realizing I had no idea where the ball was coming down.

WHAM! The football came out of nowhere, smacking me right on the bridge of my nose. My glasses went flying, and I staggered back, dazed.

"Oh, shoot!" I heard Archie yell as he came running over. "You alright, buddy?"

I blinked, clearing my vision. "I think so. Just need to find my glasses."

After a bit of searching, we found them, but one earpiece had snapped clean off, leaving a nasty cut on the side of my face.

Ron, who'd been watching from the sidelines, came jogging over with a first aid kit. "Hold still," he said, cleaning the cut and applying some butterfly bandages. "There, that should do it. Brownie, you might want to sit out the rest of practice, though."

I nodded, gingerly touching the bandages. "Yeah, I'm done catching Archie's punts. Can't see the darn things anyway."

Archie looked sheepish. "Sorry about that. Guess I don't know my strength sometimes."

I waved him off, managing a smile. "Don't worry about it. Just remind me to duck next time you're kicking."

As we headed back to the field house, I couldn't help but chuckle. It had been a long, hard summer of work and training, but moments like these—the camaraderie, the shared struggles, and triumphs—made it all worthwhile. Football season was just around the corner, and come what may, I knew we were ready for it.

Chapter 12: Living At Dusty's Home

The summer sun was beating down on us as Ron and I lugged our mattresses up the driveway of a modest-looking house.

"Remind me again how you scored this sweet gig?" I panted, adjusting my grip on the mattress.

Ron grinned, fishing a key out of his pocket. "Remember Dusty Rhodes? The manager over at Gold's Department Store downtown? Well, he's moving, and he needed someone to house-sit. Coach put in a good word for me, and here we are!"

As we stepped inside, the emptiness of the house echoed around us. Ron whistled, the sound bouncing off the bare walls. "Home sweet home, eh?"

I chuckled, dropping my mattress in what I assumed used to be the living room. "It's got a roof and walls. That's a step up from the field house floor, I'd say."

Ron nodded, wiping sweat from his brow. "You got that right. Plus, we've got a job to do. Realtor wants us to keep the yard looking sharp and keep the utilities running. Small price to pay for a place to crash, if you ask me."

Over the next few weeks, Ron and I fell into a comfortable routine. We'd wake up early, tend to the yard, then head off to our respective summer jobs. In the evenings, we'd often sit out on the porch, watching the neighborhood settle into the quiet of night.

One such evening, as we sat sipping on cold lemonades, Ron turned to me with a thoughtful expression. "You know, I've been meaning to tell you something."

I raised an eyebrow. "Oh yeah? What's on your mind, big guy?"

He took a deep breath. "Well, you remember Paula from back home?"

I nodded. "Sure, your high school sweetheart, right? She's over at Ohio University now, isn't she?"

Ron shifted in his seat, looking uncomfortable. "Well, here's the thing...Paula and I, we got married last year. My freshman year."

I nearly choked on my lemonade. "Married? You've been married this whole time?"

He nodded, a sheepish grin spreading across his face. "Yeah, we kept it under wraps. Didn't want it to interfere with my scholarship, you know?"

I shook my head, still processing the information. "Well, I'll be. You sly dog. So what now? Is Paula still at Ohio U?"

Ron's expression sobered a bit. "She had to quit. She's planning to move out here to Lincoln this fall. We're looking at renting a duplex."

I whistled low. "That's a big step, man. You sure you're ready for all that?"

He nodded, determination clear in his eyes. "We've talked it through. It won't be easy, but we're committed to making it work."

As the summer drew to a close, Ron and I packed up McDole's tiny Fiat for a road trip back to Ohio. As we squeezed into the car, I couldn't help but laugh.

"Mac, buddy, I think your side of the car is about to scrape the pavement!"

Mac grinned good-naturedly; the car noticeably lower on the driver's side because of his football player physique. "Yeah, yeah, laugh it up. At least I don't need a booster seat to see over the dashboard!"

The drive to Toledo was long but filled with laughter and easy conversation. As we crossed the state line into Ohio, I turned to Mac. "So, what's the plan once we get back?"

Mac's eyes lit up. "Well, Paula and I have found a nice little duplex. We're gonna get settled in before the fall semester starts."

I nodded, then a thought struck me. "Wait, where am I gonna live? The dorms aren't open yet."

Mac chuckled. "Don't worry, buddy. We've got a spare bedroom downstairs. If you chip in for rent, it's all yours."

Relief washed over me. "Really? Mac, you're a lifesaver."

The next few weeks were a whirlwind of activity. We helped Mac and Paula move into their new place, and I got settled into my cozy basement room. As we sat around their small kitchen table one evening, celebrating our new living arrangement, Paula dropped a bombshell.

"So," she began, a nervous smile playing on her lips, "I have some news."

Mac reached over and took her hand. "What is it, honey?"

Paula took a deep breath. "I'm pregnant."

The room fell silent for a moment before erupting in excited chatter. Mac swept Paula up in a bear hug, his face a mix of joy and shock.

"I'm gonna be a dad?" he kept repeating, as if convincing himself.

I clapped him on the back. "Congratulations, you two! This calls for a toast!"

As the fall semester began, our little household settled into a new rhythm. Paula's pregnancy progressed, and we all pitched in to help prepare for the baby's arrival. Late one night, as Mac and I were assembling a crib, he turned to me with a serious expression.

"You know, I never thought I'd be doing this at twenty. Married, baby on the way, balancing football and school. It's a lot, you know?"

I nodded, handing him a screwdriver. "I can't even imagine. But hey, you've got Paula, and you've got us. We're all in this together."

He smiled, gratitude clear in his eyes. "Thanks, man. I don't know what we'd do without you guys."

When little Tammy arrived later that year, our duplex became a hub of activity. Late-night feedings, diaper changes, and lullabies became as much a part of our routine as football practice and study sessions.

One night, as I watched Mac rock Tammy to sleep, I couldn't help but marvel at how much had changed in just a year. From living in Dusty's empty house to this moment, it had been quite a journey.

Mac caught my eye and grinned. "What are you smiling about?"

I shook my head, still smiling. "Just thinking about how life can surprise you. Here we are, a couple of college kids, and look at us now."

He nodded, looking down at his sleeping daughter. "Yeah, it's not what I expected. But you know what? I wouldn't change it for the world."

As I headed down to my room that night, I couldn't help but feel grateful. For the unexpected turns life had taken, for the friends who had become Husker family, and for the brief moments that made it all worthwhile. Who knew what the next year would bring?

Chapter 13: Getting a Job at the Administration Building

The leaves were turning as I trudged across campus, my mind heavy with the realization that my schedule this Junior semester just wouldn't mesh with my job at Russell Stover's. As I passed the student union, lost in thought, a familiar voice called out to me.

"Hey there, sugar! Why the long face?"

I looked up to see Mrs. Johnson, one of the cafeteria ladies, peering at me with concern.

"Oh, hi Mrs. Johnson," I sighed. "Just figuring out how I'm gonna make ends meet this semester. My class schedule's all over the place, and I can't keep my old job."

"Now, don't you worry. Have you tried the employment office over at the administration building? They're always looking for good workers, and they're real understanding about class schedules."

My face lit up. "Really? I hadn't even thought of that. Thanks, Mrs. Johnson!"

"Anytime, sugar," she smiled. "Now go on and see what they've got for you."

The next day, I sat in the employment office, nervously straightening my shirt as I waited for my interview. A friendly-looking man called me in, introduced himself as Mr. Thompson, and after a brief chat, he led me down to the mailroom.

"Larry," Mr. Thompson called out. "I've got a potential replacement for you here."

A lanky guy with glasses looked up from a pile of envelopes. "Oh, thank goodness," he grinned. "I was worrying I'd be stuck here past graduation."

Mr. Thompson chuckled. "Why don't you show him the ropes? If it looks like a good fit, we can get him started next week."

As Larry led me around the mailroom, explaining the sorting system and delivery routes, I couldn't help but feel a bit overwhelmed.

"Don't worry," Larry said, noticing my expression. "It looks like a lot, but you'll get the hang of it in no time. The best part is you get to know everyone in the building. Oh, and sometimes you get to play chauffeur for the Chancellor."

My eyes widened. "The Chancellor? Really?"

Larry nodded, grinning. "Yep. Don't worry, he's a nice guy. Just don't talk his ear off about football, or you'll never get him to his appointments on time."

After shadowing Larry for a day, I felt much more confident. Mr. Thompson offered me the job, and I eagerly accepted. The flexible hours were perfect for my class schedule, and the pay was better than I'd expected.

My first few weeks on the job flew by in a whirlwind of names, faces, and office numbers. I'd make my rounds twice a day, picking up and delivering mail to the various departments spread across the four-story building.

One day, as I was making my afternoon rounds, I stopped by the Housing Department. A kind-faced woman looked up as I entered, a warm smile spreading across her face.

"Well, if it isn't our new mailman," she said. "I don't think we've been properly introduced. I'm Beth."

I smiled back, oddly at ease in her presence. "Nice to meet you, Beth. I'm—"

"Oh, I know who you are, honey," she interrupted with a wink. "Word gets around. Now, why don't you tell me a bit about yourself?"

And so began my daily chats with Beth. At first, I was a bit taken aback by her interest in my life, but soon I looked forward to our conversations.

One afternoon, as I was sorting through the Housing Department's mail, Beth looked at me with a thoughtful expression.

"You know," she said, "I hope you don't mind, but I've started thinking of you as a nephew of sorts. Would it be alright if I called you my honorary nephew?"

I was touched by her words, a warm feeling spreading through my chest. "I'd like that, Beth. Does that mean I get to call you Auntie Beth?"

She beamed at me. "I'd be honored, sweetie."

From that day on, my stops at the Housing Department became the highlight of my rounds. Auntie Beth always had a kind word, a bit of advice, or just a sympathetic ear when I needed it.

One particularly rough day, after a failed exam and a misunderstanding with a professor, I trudged into her office, my shoulders slumped.

"Oh dear," Auntie Beth said, taking one look at my face. "Rough day?"

I nodded, sinking into the chair across from her desk. "You could say that."

"Want to talk about it?" she asked gently.

And so I poured out my frustrations—about the exam I'd studied so hard for but still bombed, about the professor who seemed to have it out for me, about how sometimes it all felt like too much.

Auntie Beth listened patiently, nodding along. When I finished, she leaned forward, her eyes kind but firm.

"Now you listen here, young man," she said. "Everyone has days like this. But you're smart, you're hardworking, and you've got more grit than most folks I know. This is just a bump in the road, you hear me?"

I nodded, feeling better already.

"Good," she continued. "Now, here's what we're going to do. You're going to talk to that professor, clear up any misunderstandings. And for that class you're struggling with? I happen to know a tutor who'd be perfect. I'll give you their number."

As I left her office that day, my spirits lifted and a game plan in hand, I realized just how lucky I was. Not only had I found a job that worked with my schedule, but I'd found people who cared about me—really cared.

That evening, as I walked home, I thought about how much had changed since I first arrived at the university. From Maryellen at Russell Stover's to Auntie Beth at the administration building, I'd found people who saw something in me, who believed in me.

For the first time in a long while, I felt like I truly belonged. And as I looked ahead to the rest of the semester, I knew that whatever challenges came my way, I wouldn't have to face them alone.

Chapter 14: Tending Bar at the University Club

I strolled into Auntie Beth's office one afternoon, my usual stack of mail in hand. She looked up from her desk with that warm smile I appreciated so much.

"Well, if it isn't my favorite honorary nephew," she said. "How are you doing today, sweetie?"

I shrugged, "Oh, you know, same old. I've been thinking about picking up an evening job. My schedule's a bit tight, but I could use the extra cash."

Auntie Beth's eyes lit up. "As a matter of fact, I might have just the thing for you. The University Club is looking for a bartender. It's up in the Stewart building—you know, that tall one downtown?"

The next day, I found myself in the elevator of the Stewart building, my stomach doing flips as I ascended to the top floor. The club manager, Mr. Anderson, greeted me with a firm handshake.

"So, you're Beth's boy," he said, looking me up and down. "Let's chat a bit, shall we?"

After a brief interview, Mr. Anderson nodded approvingly. "Alright, let's introduce you to June. She'll be the one to really decide if you're a good fit."

June Kruger was a force of nature. A petite woman with light graying hair and sharp green eyes, she was slender and about my height. she sized me up the moment I walked behind the bar.

"Ever been a bartender before?" she asked, her tone no-nonsense.

I shook my head. "No, ma'am."

She nodded, as if that's exactly what she expected. "Alright, here's the deal. You come in tomorrow, and I'll show you the ropes. You'll need to be here evenings until 11:00 or 12:00. Some members like to come up after town functions for a nightcap. I'll teach you how to close down. And we'll need you here at 11:00 a.m. for the lunch crowd, 11:30 to 2:30. Can you swing that with your classes?"

I quickly ran through my schedule in my head. "I can make it by 11:00 on Mondays, Wednesdays, and Fridays. Tuesdays and Thursdays, I can be here by 12:30."

June nodded, seemingly satisfied. "Good. You'll work the noon crowd with me, then handle the evening shift solo. I leave around 5:30. You'll serve dinner drinks, after-dinner drinks, then stick around for any walk-ins. When it's slow, feel free to study. Just make sure you lock up the back bar with the plywood board every night."

Over the next few weeks, I fell into a rhythm. June was a patient teacher, showing me how to mix drinks, handle difficult customers, and keep the bar running smoothly. One quiet evening, as I was polishing glasses, she surprised me with a compliment.

"You know, Jim," she said, "I'm glad you're here. The last guy, Melvin, he was a real piece of work. Always late if he showed up at all. And I'm pretty sure he was taking bottles home with him every night."

I felt a surge of pride at her words. "Thanks, June. I really appreciate the opportunity."

A couple months into the job, June presented me with a wrapped package about three feet tall.

"Happy birthday, kid," she said gruffly, but I could see the warmth in her eyes.

I pulled off the paper and to my surprise, it was a new, small bicycle with a banana seat.

"June, this is amazing! Thank you so much! I don't have to walk back and forth from school and my apartment. The time I will save will be great."

She waved off my thanks. "Just make sure you're not late for your shifts," she said, but I could see she was pleased.

That bike became my main mode of transportation. I'd ride it to school, then to the Stewart building, taking it up in the elevator to the fourteenth floor.

"Top floor, please," I'd say to the elevator operator, my bike balanced precariously beside me.

One evening, as I was setting up for the dinner crowd, Mr. Anderson approached the bar.

"Jim, my boy," he said, clapping me on the shoulder. "I just wanted to let you know that the bar's profits have seen a significant uptick since you started. And I've been hearing good things from the members about you. I want you to go out and find some good music records and a record player to place in the bar area."

I couldn't help but beam with pride. "Thank you, sir. I'm really enjoying the work."

As the months went by, I found myself truly appreciating the job. The free meal each evening was a godsend for a broke college student, and I struck up a friendship with Mike McCarthy, the head chef. He was a top chef trained in Los Angeles but could not adjust to big city living. He moved back to Lincoln to be at home.

"Prime rib again, Jim?" he'd tease as I picked up my dinner.

"What can I say, Mike? You've ruined me for all other food," I'd joke back.

But perhaps the most valuable aspect of the job was the people skills I was developing. Night after night, I found myself conversing with some of the most important people in Lincoln—professors, businessmen, politicians. At first, I was terrified, stumbling over my words and avoiding eye contact.

One night, a regular—Dr. Thompson from the Economics department—noticed my discomfort.

"You know, son," he said, leaning on the bar, "the key to a good conversation is eye contact. It shows you're engaged, that you're really listening."

I nodded, forcing myself to meet his gaze. "Like this, sir?"

He smiled. "Exactly. Now, tell me about your studies. What's your major?"

From that night on, I attempted to improve my conversational skills. I learned to listen actively, to ask thoughtful questions, and to hold my own in discussions on topics ranging from local politics to international affairs.

As I locked up the bar one night, nearly a year into the job, I reflected on how much I'd grown. From the nervous kid who could barely mix a drink, I'd become a confident bartender, trusted by my colleagues and respected by the club members.

I thought about Auntie Beth, and how her simple act of kindness in recommending me for this job had opened up so many opportunities. I made a mental note to thank her again the next time I saw her.

As I rode my bike home through the quiet streets of Lincoln, I felt a sense of accomplishment and gratitude. This job was more than just a way to make ends meet—it shaped me and prepared me for the future in ways I never could have anticipated. And for that, I was truly thankful.

Chapter 15: How I Became Rich from What I Experienced

One quiet evening at the University Club, as I was polishing glasses and reflecting on the various members I knew, a realization struck me. I'd been exposed to a cross-section of Lincoln's most successful individuals, and I couldn't help but wonder what was their secret? How had they achieved such wealth and status?

As if reading my thoughts, Mr. Jameson, one of our regular patrons and a successful businessman, settled onto a barstool.

"Penny for your thoughts, Jim?" he asked, his eyes twinkling with curiosity.

I hesitated for a moment before responding. "Well, Mr. Jameson, I was just thinking about success. About how to become...well, rich."

He chuckled, not unkindly. "Ah, the eternal question. And what conclusions have you drawn, young man?"

I set down the glass I'd been polishing and leaned on the bar, warming to the topic. "Well, from what I've seen here at the club, it seems there are really only three main paths to wealth."

Mr. Jameson raised an eyebrow, intrigued. "Do tell."

"First," I began, ticking off on my fingers, "you can inherit it. But that's not an option for everyone. Certainly not for me—I don't exactly come from money."

Mr. Jameson nodded thoughtfully. "True enough. What's your second path?"

"Owning your own business," I continued. "But again, that requires startup capital and know-how that I just don't have right now."

"Astute observation," Mr. Jameson said. "And the third?"

I straightened up, feeling more confident. "The third path, and the one that seems most accessible to me, is becoming a top-notch salesman. Selling a product you believe in, something that can really make a difference in people's lives."

Mr. Jameson's eyes lit up. "Now you're onto something, Jim. Sales is indeed a powerful path to success. But tell me, what makes you think this is the right path for you?"

I gestured around the club. "Well, I've seen it firsthand here. We have members who've made their fortunes selling life insurance, real estate, you name it. They all seem to have one thing in common—they're great at connecting with people and they truly believe in what they're selling."

Just then, another regular, Mrs. Thompson, a successful life insurance agent, approached the bar. "I couldn't help but overhear," she said with a smile. "Jim, are you considering a career in sales?"

I nodded, feeling sheepish. "I'm thinking about it, Mrs. Thompson. It seems like a viable path to success."

She nodded approvingly. "It can be, if you're willing to put in the work. But let me tell you, it's not just about the product. It's about building relationships, understanding people's needs, and genuinely wanting to help them."

Mr. Jameson chimed in, "Absolutely right, Margaret. Jim, you've already got a head start on that front. I've watched you these past months, how you interact with the members here. You've got a natural talent for putting people at ease and really listening to them."

I felt a warmth spread through my chest at their words. "Thank you both. That means a lot coming from you."

Mrs. Thompson leaned in, her voice taking on a mentoring tone. "Now, if you're serious about this, you need to start thinking about what kind of product or service you'd want to represent. It has to be something you're passionate about, something you'd be proud to stand behind."

I nodded, my mind already racing with possibilities. "I'll definitely give that some thought, Mrs. Thompson. Thank you for the advice."

As the night wore on and I closed up the bar, I couldn't stop thinking about our conversation. The path ahead seemed clearer now, more tangible. I may not have had a fortune to inherit or the means to start my own business just yet, but I had something valuable—the experiences and lessons I'd gained from my time at the University Club.

I realized that every interaction, every conversation I'd had with the members, had been preparing me for this potential future. I'd learned how to read people, how to engage them in meaningful conversation, how to make them feel valued and understood. These were all skills that could serve me well in a sales career.

As I rode my bike home that night, the cool evening air clearing my head, I felt a sense of excitement and purpose. I may not know exactly what product or service I'd end up selling, but I knew I was on the right track. The wealth and success I'd observed at the University Club no longer seemed like an unattainable dream, but a future—one I was determined to work toward.

I made a mental note to start paying even closer attention to the successful salespeople among our members, to learn from their techniques and strategies. And perhaps, I thought with a smile, I might even ask Mrs. Thompson or Mr. Jameson for some mentoring advice.

The future was still uncertain, but for the first time, I felt like I had a roadmap to success. And it all started with the lessons I'd learned behind that bar at the University Club.

Chapter 16: Salesman Encouragement

As my third year of college drew to a close, I stood at a crossroads. The decision to pursue a career in sales was solidifying in my mind, but the path forward still seemed hazy. When I heard about the University's annual job fair for graduates, I knew this was my chance to take the first step toward my future.

The day of the fair arrived, and I found myself in a sea of suits and nervous energy. The gymnasium had been transformed into a bustling marketplace of opportunity, with company booths lining the walls and snaking through the center of the room. I took a deep breath, straightened my tie (borrowed from Ron for the occasion), and dove in.

I spoke with representatives from several companies, but one stood out to me—Procter & Gamble. Their booth was sleek and professional, staffed by recruiters with bright smiles and firm handshakes. I approached, my heart pounding but my resolve firm.

"Good morning," I said to the recruiter, a man in his forties with kind eyes and salt-and-pepper hair. "I'm interested in learning more about sales opportunities with P&G."

The recruiter, whose name tag read 'Mr. Thompson', smiled warmly. "Excellent! Why don't you start by filling out this application? Then we can chat a bit."

I nodded, taking the clipboard he offered. I found a quiet corner and began filling out the form, my pen hovering for a moment over each question before I committed my answer to paper. When I reached the section about my college experience, I paused. There was a box asking how much money I had earned toward my degree. I thought about all the jobs I'd worked—Russell Stover's, the mail room, the University Club—and carefully calculated the total. It was with a sense of pride that I wrote "100%" in that box.

Returning to Mr. Thompson, I handed over my completed application. He glanced over it, his eyebrows rising slightly as he reached the education section. Then he looked up at me, his expression unreadable.

"Well, Jim," he said, "why don't you tell me a bit about why you're interested in sales?"

For the next twenty minutes, we talked about my experiences, my motivations, and my goals. I told him about my time at the University Club, about the successful salespeople I'd met there and the lessons I'd learned from them. As our conversation drew to a close, Mr. Thompson leaned back in his chair, a thoughtful expression on his face.

"Thank you for your time, Jim," he said. "I'd like you to come back and see me in two days, at 10:00 a.m. sharp. Can you do that?"

I nodded eagerly, "Absolutely, Mr. Thompson. I'll be here."

The next two days crawled by as my mind buzzed with possibilities. When the appointed time arrived, I was outside Mr. Thompson's temporary office five minutes early, my palms sweaty but my resolve firm.

"Come in, Jim," Mr. Thompson called when I knocked. As I settled into the chair across from him, I noticed a familiar application on his desk—mine.

Mr. Thompson folded his hands on the desk, his expression serious. "Jim, I want to be straight with you. I will not be hiring you for P&G at this time."

My heart sank, but before I could respond, he held up a hand.

"However," he continued, "I want to talk to you about something else. In your interview, you mentioned you owe your ability to attend college to your high school friends. You said they were very important to you."

I nodded, unsure where this was going.

Mr. Thompson picked up my application. "Jim, I've been doing this job for twelve years. In all that time, I have never—not once—seen someone write 100 percent in this box." He tapped the section about money earned toward my degree. "Never. Do you understand how remarkable that is?"

I felt a flush of pride, mixed with embarrassment. "I...I just wrote down what was true, sir."

He nodded, a slight smile playing at the corners of his mouth. "Exactly. And that's why I wanted to talk to you today. Jim, I want you to leave here with this thought: You owe nothing to your friends."

I must have looked confused because he continued, his voice gentle but firm. "Your friends opened a door for you, yes. But you, Jim, you're the one who walked through that door. You're the one who's been working multiple jobs, studying late into the night, pushing yourself to succeed. That's all you."

His words hit me like a ton of bricks. I'd been so focused on my gratitude to my friends that I'd discounted my own efforts.

"You need to be proud of what you're doing," Mr. Thompson continued. "Yes, be grateful for the opportunities you've been given, but also acknowledge your own hard work and determination. That's what will make you successful in sales—or in any career you choose."

I sat there, stunned, as his words sank in. For so long, I'd felt like I was just barely keeping my head above water, always owing someone for my next breath. But Mr. Thompson was right—I had worked hard. I had earned my place here.

"Thank you, Mr. Thompson," I said. "I...I think I needed to hear that."

He smiled, warm and genuine. "I'm glad, Jim. Now, as I previously mentioned, I'm not recommending you for a position with P&G, but I want you to come back after you graduate. With your work ethic and your ability to connect with people, I think you could go far in sales. Just remember—you're not just opening doors for yourself anymore. You're building the entire house."

As I left the office, I felt like a weight had been lifted from my shoulders. For the first time, I truly believed I could succeed in sales—not because of who I knew or what doors had been opened for me, but because of who I was and what I had accomplished.

Walking across the sun-drenched quad, I made a silent promise to myself. I would continue to be grateful for the help I'd received, but I would also recognize my own worth, my own efforts. And when I returned to that job fair next year, diploma in hand, I would do so not as someone who owed the world, but as someone ready to make his mark on it.

The path ahead was still long, and I knew there would be challenges. But for perhaps the first time, I felt truly ready to face them. The salesman I wanted to become wasn't just a distant dream anymore—he was right here, walking across this campus, ready to take on the world.

Chapter 17: The McDole Apartment Chronicles

The crisp autumn air carried a sense of change as I stood on the steps of McDole's apartment, key in hand. Ron and Paula, with their new baby, had packed up for St. Louis, where Ron was starting his NFL career with the Cardinals. Their departure left me with both an opportunity and a challenge.

"You sure you're up for this, Jim?" Ron had asked as he handed over the keys. "Finding renters, managing the place...it's a lot of responsibility."

I'd nodded, projecting more confidence than I felt. "Don't worry, I've got this. You guys focus on St. Louis. We'll take good care of the place until spring."

Now, standing alone in the furnished apartment, the magnitude of the task ahead hit me. I needed to find roommates, and fast, to cover the rent and keep the place running smoothly. The echo of my footsteps in the empty rooms seemed to mock my confidence.

My first call was to an old friend from my freshman year, Dale Seimer. I found him at the small school in Roka where he was coaching football and track.

"Dale," I said when he picked up, "how do you feel about becoming roommates again?"

A chuckle was heard on the other end of the line. "Jim, my man! Are you serious? What's the deal?"

I explained the situation with McDole's apartment. "It's a great place, Dale. We just need to find a few more guys to split the rent. What do you say?"

"Count me in," Dale replied without hesitation. "And I might know a guy. Remember Carol Zuba, the fullback from a couple of years ago? He might be interested."

With Dale on board, things looked up. But we still needed two more roommates to make the finances work. That's when I took a chance and placed an ad in the Lincoln Star.

The day after the ad ran, our first potential roommate showed up. Dave Cook was a wiry wrestler from New York, all blonde hair, and East Coast charm.

"So, this is the place, huh?" Dave said, looking around with an appraising eye. "Not bad, not bad at all. What's the deal with rent and food?"

I laid out the financial arrangement, including our plan for a communal food pool. Dave's eyes lit up. He stated that he received a $300 monthly allowance from his father.

"My old man owns three button factories back east," he explained. "Figures this allowance will teach me financial responsibility or something. Count me in, fellas. I make a mean mac and cheese."

With the three of us locked in, we just needed one more roommate to make the numbers work. That's when Eldon Poppe answered our ad. He showed up one evening after work, still in his suit from his job at the Capitol building.

"I hope I'm not too late," Eldon said, slightly out of breath. "I just saw the ad today and came straight over."

We gave him a tour of the apartment, explaining our setup. When we mentioned the food pool, Eldon's eyes lit up.

"I'm a whiz with grocery shopping on a budget," he said. "Comes with working in the Highway Department. We're always looking for ways to stretch a dollar."

And just like that, our motley crew was complete. We gathered in the living room that first night, each of us bringing something to contribute to our first shared meal.

"Alright, gentlemen," I said, looking around at my new roommates. "Let's lay down some ground rules. First up, the food pool. We each put in $25 every two weeks. Agreed?"

There were nods all around. Dave piped up, "Eldon and I can handle the grocery runs. I've got a car, and with his budgeting skills, we'll eat like kings."

Dale chimed in, "Carol and I can take care of the cooking. Between the two of us, we should be able to whip up some decent meals."

"Great," I said. "Dave, Eldon, and I will handle clean-up duty and keep the place tidy. Sound fair to everyone?"

The arrangement settled, we dug into our improvised dinner. As we ate and chatted, I could feel a sense of camaraderie developing. We were an odd mix—a football coach, a wrestler, a government worker, and Carol, the truck driver, along with me, the aspiring bartender—but somehow, it felt right.

Over the next few weeks, we settled into a rhythm. True to their word, Dave and Eldon became masters of budget shopping, often returning from grocery runs with triumphant grins and bags full of deals.

"You won't believe what we found on sale," Dave would announce, holding up a case of macaroni and cheese like it was a trophy.

Dale and Carol turned out to be decent cooks, transforming our budget ingredients into hearty meals that kept us all well-fed. The apartment was often filled with the aroma of their latest culinary experiments.

"Hope you boys are hungry," Dale would call out as we returned home in the evenings. "Carol's whipped up something special tonight."

As for Dave, Eldon, and myself, we tackled the clean-up with gusto. There was something satisfying about maintaining our shared space, keeping it ready for the next meal or study session.

One evening, as we all sat around the living room, full of dinner and laughing at one of Dave's outrageous stories about the New York button industry, I caught myself feeling a sense of contentment. This arrangement, born out of necessity, had turned into something more—a family.

"You know," Eldon said during a lull in the conversation, "I was worried about finding a place to live when I first moved here for the job. But this...this is better than I could have hoped for."

There were murmurs of agreement around the room. Dale raised his glass in a toast.

"To unlikely roommates and unexpected friendships."

As we clinked our glasses together, I thought about Ron and Paula in St. Louis. I hoped they were settling in as well as we had here. When they returned in the spring, they'd find their apartment well-cared for, filled with the echoes of the life we'd built here.

The months ahead would bring their challenges, I was sure. But looking around at this group—my motley crew of roommates—I felt ready to face whatever came our way. We'd found more than just a place to live; we'd found a home.

Chapter 18: Bunnies, Blunders, and Bloody Marys

The crisp winter air nipped at our faces as Dave Cook, Ed Johnson, Dale Seimer, and I piled into Dave's car, our spirits high with anticipation. Chicago awaited us, promising a New Year's Eve we'd never forget.

"You guys ready for this?" Dave grinned, starting the engine. "My uncle's got us hooked up at the Playboy Club."

Ed leaned forward from the backseat, a hint of worry in his voice. "Hey, Jim, you think twenty bucks is enough for this trip?"

I chuckled, patting my pocket. "Ed, I've got a grand total of a dollar and a quarter. Trust me, you're golden."

Little did we know just how golden Dave's uncle's connections would turn out.

The drive to Dave's grandmother's summer home on Long Lake flew by in a blur of excited chatter and plans for the big night. As we pulled up to the quaint lakeside cottage, Dave turned to us with a mischievous glint in his eye. We had two days before New Year's Eve, so the first night, Dave announced that his uncle also had a membership in the Gaslight Club, which was located in downtown Chicago.

We got all dressed up with sport coats and ties. Dave drove us into Chicago and parked in the Gaslight Club's special parking lot. Dave showed his uncle's membership card at the special peep-hole door. We were ushered into the main dining room.

Dave said, "Order anything on the menu along with drinks. My uncle said to have fun tonight. We have two floors to go for entertainment and more drinks."

***

We got home late that night and woke up the next morning with hangovers and alcohol breath. We laid around all day watching the Bowl games on TV.

Late that afternoon, Dave announced, "Alright, fellas. Get yourselves pretty. We're hitting the Playboy Club tonight! It's New Year's Eve."

The club was a marvel of luxury and excitement. As we entered, Dave flashed his uncle's membership card, and suddenly, we were in a world of glamour and sophistication.

"Remember," Dave whispered as we headed to the first floor, "everything goes on the card. It's a dollar fifty per charge, per person, per floor."

The first floor was a pool player's paradise. Bunnies in their iconic outfits sashayed around, delivering drinks and smiles in equal measure.

"Seven and Seven," Dale ordered, eyeing an attractive bunny. "When in Rome, right?"

As the night progressed, we ascended through the club's levels, each floor offering new delights. The second floor's dining room was a gastronomic wonderland.

"I'll have the prime rib," I declared, feeling like a million bucks. "And another Seven and Seven, please."

By the time we reached the third floor, the clock ticking closer to midnight; we were all feeling the effects of our revelry. The atmosphere was electric, the drinks flowing freely.

That's when things took a turn.

In a moment of drunken foolishness, Dale reached out and yanked down the front of a bunny's uniform. The poor girl stood there, exposed and shocked, as I quickly grabbed her tray of drinks to prevent a catastrophe.

"Oh shit," Dave muttered, quickly turning the bunny around to help her cover up.

The floor manager appeared as if by magic, his face a mask of controlled fury. "Gentlemen, I'm going to have to ask you to leave."

Chastened and stumbling, we made our way out onto the bustling Chicago streets just before midnight. The city was alive with celebration, and we soon found ourselves swept up in the New Year's festivities.

"Happy New Year!" we shouted as the clock struck twelve, our earlier mishap momentarily forgotten in the sea of revelers.

The drive back to the lake house in the wee hours of the morning was a quiet affair. Most of us passed out while Dave, the lone sober one, navigated the dark roads.

The next day dawned bright and painful. We nursed our hangovers with Bloody Marys, sprawled around the living room watching football.

"Anyone remember how we got home?" Ed groaned, holding an ice pack to his head.

Dave, looking annoyingly chipper, laughed. "Let's just say it's a good thing one of us can hold his liquor."

As the others headed back to Lincoln the next day, Dave and I stayed on. We returned to the Playboy Club night after night. We befriended Sonny King, a stand-up comedian after his performance on the third floor. He regaled us with tales of his performances in Omaha in years past.

"You boys remind me of myself at your age," Sonny chuckled one night. "Just try not to get thrown out of any more clubs, alright?"

When we finally returned to Lincoln, we felt exhausted but exhilarated. It wasn't until later that Dave dropped the bombshell.

"You guys won't believe this," he said, his eyes wide. "The bill for New Year's Eve alone was three hundred dollars!"

We all winced, thinking of Dave's uncle who also had memberships in the Gaslight Club and the Playboy Club. But as we looked at each other, we couldn't help but burst into laughter. It had been an adventure we'd never forget; a story we'd tell for years to come.

As I headed back to my regular college routine, I couldn't help but smile. Who would have thought that a dollar and a quarter could buy such an unforgettable experience? Chicago, the Playboy Club, and that fateful New Year's Eve would forever be etched in my memory—a reminder of the wild, wonderful unpredictability of youth.

Chapter 19: Shenanigans at Lake Okoboji

Well, let me tell you about the time me and the boys decided to shake off the winter blues with a little adventure down at Lake Okoboji. It was Easter break, and we were itching to get out of Lincoln and into some trouble—the good kind, mind you.

First things first, I had to sweet-talk June Kroger at the University Club into giving me a week off. Bless her heart, she didn't put up much of a fuss. With that settled, I rounded up the usual suspects: my roommates Dave Cook and Dale Seimer, plus our buddies Gary Warden and a fella we called Oggie Doggie. Now, Oggie had just bought himself a fancy ski boat with a trailer, and we were all raring to try it out.

We piled into a car, hooked up that boat, and hit the road for Iowa. The drive was a hoot, with Gary belting out off-key country tunes and Oggie regaling us with tales of his latest romantic conquests—most of which we took with a grain of salt, if you catch my drift.

When we rolled into Okoboji, we found ourselves a cozy little motel on the outskirts of town. Nothing fancy, mind you, but it had beds and a roof, which was all we really needed. We unhooked the trailer and painted the town red—or at least gave it a light coating of pink.

Downtown Okoboji was something else. They had themselves a permanent carnival right smack in the middle of everything. Ferris wheels, cotton candy stands, the works. But before we got too carried away, our grumbling stomachs led us to a local joint for some grub.

After filling our bellies, we moseyed on over to the carnival. That's when Gary spotted it—the Hammerhead. Now, let me paint you a picture of this contraption. Imagine a giant hammer, but instead of a flat head, it's got these bullet-shaped cages attached. Two seats in each cage, one in front and one in back. The whole thing swings up into the air, flips you upside down, and brings you back down faster than a hot knife through butter.

Gary's eyes lit up like a kid on Christmas morning. He was bound and determined to ride that thing with each of us. Dale, being the sensible one, politely declined. But the rest of us? Well, we were young and dumb enough to give it a whirl.

The fella running the ride strapped us in tight and locked that cage down over our heads. Then, without so much as a "hold on to your britches," he set that thing in motion. Up we went, swinging back and forth, higher and higher. Just when you thought you couldn't go any further, he'd stop us right at the top, leaving us dangling upside down like bats in a cave.

Now, Oggie Doggie wasn't too keen on riding, but we talked him into it. Big mistake. About the second time around, poor Oggie lost his dinner—while he was upside down, no less. By some miracle, he kept it off his clothes, but the ride operator had to stop and let him off. A couple of us had to half-carry him back to the car.

We called it a night after that, heading back to the motel to polish off the beer we'd brought along. The next morning, we were up with the sun, ready to try out Oggie's new boat. We spent the whole day taking turns water skiing, whooping and hollering like a bunch of cowboys at a rodeo. The lake was cool and refreshing, and for a few hours, we felt like kings of the world.

That evening, after we'd showered off the lake water and filled our bellies again, we found ourselves in a local watering hole. This place had a couple of pool tables, and we got to chatting with some locals. One fella about our age let us in on a little secret. He said, "Boys, there's a tradition in this bar. Anyone who wants to play pool has to holler 'timber' before they break."

Well, Gary, never one to back down from a challenge, stepped up to the table. Just as he was about to break, he let out a "TIMBER!"

loud enough to wake the dead. Next thing we knew, the bartender was bringing over a round of beers for everyone in the joint. Turns out, shouting "timber" meant you were buying a round for the house. At ten cents a glass, it only set Gary back a buck fifty, but boy, did we have fun with that for the rest of the night.

We kept that game going all evening, telling every newcomer about the "timber" tradition. We got ourselves a few free beers out of it too. The locals seemed to get a kick out of us city boys, and before long, we were swapping stories and laughing like old friends.

Later that night, we headed back to the carnival for another go on the Hammerhead. That's when things got fuzzy for me. I had to take a bathroom break and somehow got separated from the guys. By the time I made it back to the ride, they were gone—along with our car.

So there I was, half-seas over and facing a long walk back to the motel. As I was stumbling through a parking lot, I tripped over one of those concrete parking bumpers. Down I went, face-first. Smashed my nose something awful and broke my glasses. The temple piece got driven right into the side of my face. Thank goodness I had a handkerchief to mop up the blood.

I kept on walking, feeling pretty sorry for myself, when nature called again. I ducked behind a bush in someone's yard to relieve myself. That's when I spotted it—a milk truck, just sitting there with the doors wide open. Now, I'm not proud of what happened next, but in my addled state, it seemed like a good idea.

I climbed up into that truck and, lo-and-behold, the keys were right there in the ignition. Without thinking it through, I fired up that engine and took off down the road. I drove right past our motel and parked it a block away. Then I turned off the engine, left the keys in the ignition, and hoofed it back to our room.

The boys were mighty surprised to see me. I told them about borrowing the milk truck, but they didn't believe a word of it. I was too exhausted to argue, so I just climbed into bed and fell asleep. The next morning, nursing one heck of a hangover, I had some explaining to do—both to my buddies and to the local sheriff who came knocking about a missing milk truck.

We spent the rest of the trip lying low, doing more water skiing and hanging out at the Timber Bar. When it was time to head home, we packed up Oggie's boat and hit the road back to Lincoln, nursing our sunburns and swapping stories about our wild week at Lake Okoboji.

You know, looking back on it now, I reckon we were lucky we didn't end up in more trouble than we did. But I'll tell you what—that Easter break is still one of my favorite memories from my college days. Sometimes, it's the crazy, unplanned adventures that stick with you the longest.

Chapter 20: Hay Bales, Wrestlers, and Small-Town Charm

Well, let me tell you about the summer I spent in Osage, Iowa. It was a time I'll never forget, full of characters and experiences that you just can't make up.

It all started after I pulled my grades up enough to dodge summer school. Some of my buddies weren't so lucky, but that's what you get for spending more time at the pool hall than the library, I reckon. Anyway, my friend Harry Thompson—a real bruiser of a fella and champion wrestler for Nebraska—asked if I wanted to tag along with him to his hometown of Osage for the summer. Now, Harry and I had taken a bunch of classes together and ran in the same circles, so I figured why not? A change of scenery might do me good.

Harry came from a big family—five or six brothers, if I remember right. But that summer, it was just going to be Harry, his youngest brother Bert, and their folks at home. When we rolled into Osage, Harry's first order of business was to say howdy to his parents. His mama was sweet as pie and seemed tickled pink to have her boy home from school.

After the family reunion, Harry was itching to see his old pal, Joe Fox. Now, Joe was quite the character. He'd been a champion wrestler too, in the lightweight division for Iowa State. But life had thrown him a curveball recently—poor Joe had been in a nasty car wreck and had his jaw wired shut. You'd think that'd slow a fella down, but not Joe.

That very evening, we all moseyed down to the local watering hole. Joe, bless his heart, couldn't eat a lick of solid food, but that didn't stop him from joining in the fun. He'd brought along a bunch of long-neck beers, and I'll be darned if he didn't figure out how to drink 'em through his wired-up jaw. It was a sight to see, let me tell you.

The next day, Harry had to go interview for a summer job with the city. Joe, not one to sit idle, asked if I wanted to tag along with him to the Mayo Clinic. He had to drive up there—about eighty miles—to check on how his jaw was healing. Now, I'd never been to the famous Mayo Clinic, so I agreed.

That car ride was an adventure in itself. Every time a bird would fly across the road in front of us, Joe would duck down below the steering wheel, quick as a jackrabbit. After about the third time, I had to ask what in tarnation he was doing.

Joe got a serious look on his face and said, "Well, you see, I've got a bit of a thing about birds." He told me this story about when he was just a little tyke. His older brother Ed, in a moment of brotherly torment, had thrown a rooster at him. That ornery bird latched onto poor Joe's face with its claws and started flapping its wings something fierce. Little Joe went down like a sack of potatoes, and it took Ed a hot minute to pry that rooster off. Ever since then, Joe couldn't help but flinch at the sight of any feathered friend.

I tried not to laugh, but the mental image of Joe, this tough-as-nails wrestler, getting taken down by a rooster was just too much. We had a good chuckle about it all the way to Rochester.

Back in Osage, Harry's mama had been busy trying to find me some work. She'd put an ad in the local paper, bless her heart, saying she had a young man looking for a summer job. Harry lucked out and got himself a gig with the city water department. They were putting in a new water main, right through the middle of town—a job that'd keep him busy all summer long.

As for me, well, opportunity came knocking in the form of a local farmer. Harry's mama got a call saying he needed someone to stack baled hay in his barn for a few days. Now, I'd never worked on a farm before, but I figured it couldn't be too hard. Boy, was I in for a surprise.

Harry drove me out to the farm the next morning. The farmer looked me up and down, probably wondering if this city boy could handle the work. He pointed me toward the hayloft and explained they had a conveyor belt running from the ground up to the loft door.

Let me tell you, stacking hay bales is no picnic. It's hot, dusty work, and those bales are a lot heavier than they look. By lunchtime, I was sweating buckets and my arms felt like lead. The farmer's wife, bless her, brought out some sandwiches and the coldest lemonade I'd ever tasted. I drank a gallon of the stuff.

As I was sitting there, catching my breath, I got to thinking about how different this was from my life back in Lincoln. Here I was, in the middle of nowhere Iowa, stacking hay and rubbing elbows with wrestlers and farmers. It was a far cry from my usual summer of loafing around and picking up a few shifts at the movie theater.

The next couple of days were more of the same—wake up at the crack of dawn, head out to the farm, and stack hay until I thought my arms would fall off. But you know what? There was something satisfying about it. It was the farmer's approving nod at the end of each day, or the way Harry's mama fussed over me at dinner, making sure I ate enough to "keep my strength up."

As I lay in bed each night, muscles aching but feeling oddly content, I realized this summer in Osage was teaching me more than I'd learned in an entire semester of classes. It was about hard work, sure, but also about community, about lending a hand where it's needed, and about the kinds of friendships that can form in the most unexpected places.

Looking back now, I can say that summer in Osage was one of the best in my life. It might not have been glamorous, but it was real. And sometimes, that's all you need.

Chapter 21: A City Boy's Baptism in the Barn Loft

Let me tell you about my initiation into farm life—two days in a hayloft that felt like two years. Now, I thought I knew what hard work was, but boy, did I have another think coming.

I stood at those hayloft doors, watching the farmer and his crew work like a well-oiled machine. The tractor pulled a flatbed wagon 'round the field, while one fella scooped up bales from the ground and another stacked 'em neat as you please. Three bales high they went, till that wagon was groaning under the weight of forty-plus bales.

When they pulled into the barnyard, I knew my work was about to begin. They started feeding those bales onto the conveyor belt, and up they came to me. Now, each of those bales weighed a good fifty pounds or more. I grabbed my hay hook, feeling mighty proud of myself, and started dragging the first bale to the back of the barn.

Well, by the time I got back to the conveyor, there were already three more bales piled up in the loft. I realized right quick that my grand plan of dragging each bale to the back wasn't gonna cut it. So, I switched gears and started piling them up around the conveyor belt.

I figured I had about thirty to forty-five minutes before the next load came in. It was plenty of time to stack these bales nice and neat, right? Wrong. I underestimated just how fast those farm boys worked. No sooner had I finished stacking than I turned around to see the farmer and his sons already loading up the conveyor again.

Now, let me paint you a picture of what it's like in that hayloft. It's hot. And when I say hot, I mean the heat that makes you think you might've died and gone to the wrong place, if you catch my drift. It was a hundred degrees outside, but inside that barn? Lord have mercy, it must've been pushing a hundred and twenty.

I kept at it, pulling and stacking, pulling and stacking. My shirt, soaked through, stuck to me like a second skin. Just when I thought I couldn't take another minute, I heard the farmer holler up that it was lunchtime. I nearly cried with relief.

Walking over to the farmhouse, I spotted a big old shade tree, and under it, a spread that would make your mouth water just to look at it. The farmer's wife had laid out a feast—fried chicken, corn on the cob, and more fixings than you could shake a stick at. And the iced tea? Well, I reckon I drank my weight in it.

That kind woman must've seen how wrung out I was, 'cause she handed me a bag of ice water to take back up to the loft. I could've hugged her right then and there.

After lunch, it was back to the grind. Up in that loft, I had a bird's-eye view of the whole operation. Looking out over that alfalfa field, I could see we'd only cleared about half of it. That meant another full day of this ahead of me. I won't lie. My heart sank a little at the thought.

When five o'clock finally rolled around, I was more than ready to call it a day. Mrs. Thompson, bless her, came to pick me up. Back at the house, I hardly made it through supper before I headed for the shower. I told everyone I was turning in early, and I swear I was asleep before my head hit the pillow.

Next morning, Mrs. Thompson was shaking me awake at the crack of dawn. After a hearty breakfast, she drove me back out to the farm. This time, I came prepared with plenty of water and a pair of leather gloves. Let me tell you, those gloves were a game-changer.

Day two was more of the same—endless bales of hay, sweat pouring off me like I was standing under a waterfall. But you know what? There was something satisfying about it all. Maybe it was seeing the neat stacks of hay growing higher and higher, or maybe it was knowing I was doing something real, something tangible.

By the end of that second day, we'd filled that barn to the rafters. We stacked and stored every last bale, ready for the long winter ahead. I ached in places I didn't even know could ache, but there was a sense of pride there too.

Mrs. Thompson came to pick me up again, this time with a check in hand for my labor. As I climbed into her car, muscles screaming in protest, the farmer gave me a nod. Just a nod, mind you, but coming from him, it felt like high praise.

On the drive back, Mrs. Thompson asked how it went. I opened my mouth to complain about the heat, the endless bales, the backbreaking work. But what came out instead was, "It was good, ma'am. Real good."

And you know what? It was. Those two days in that hayloft taught me more about hard work and perseverance than any classroom ever could. It wasn't glamorous. It wasn't easy, but it was honest work. The kind of work that leaves you bone-tired but satisfied.

Looking back now, that summer job was more than just a way to earn some cash. It was a glimpse into a way of life I'd never known before. A life where the day's success is measured in sweat and calluses, where a job well done means food on the table and hay in the barn.

I may have started that job as a city boy, but I left with a new respect for farmers and the work they do. And let me tell you, I've never looked at a bale of hay the same way since. Every time I pass a hay field now, I give a little nod of respect. 'Cause I know firsthand what goes into getting that hay from field to barn.

That summer in Osage, up in that sweltering hayloft, I learned the value of hard work, the satisfaction of a job well done, and the simple pleasure of a cold glass of iced tea at the end of a long, hot day. And you know what? I wouldn't trade that experience for all the air conditioning in the world.

Chapter 22: The Summer That Changed Everything

I reckon I'd overstayed my welcome at Harry's place, but his mama was sweet as pie about it. After a week, I figured it was high time to mosey on. That's when I remembered good ol' Larry Kramer, that football guard for Nebraska. Larry lived in Austin, Minnesota. Before I left for Osage, Larry had asked me to come home with him for the summer.

I rang him up one evening, twirling the phone cord 'round my finger. "Hey Larry, it's me. How's life treating ya up there in Austin?"

"Well, if it ain't my old buddy!" Larry's voice boomed through the receiver. "Life's good, but Daddy's got me working like a dog. Says the house needs painting."

"That so?" I chuckled. "Sounds like quite the summer project."

"You bet. Say, ain't you supposed to be heading up this way? Joe Fox mentioned you might be passing through on his way to Mayo's."

I nodded, forgetting he couldn't see me. "That's right. Got any room for a wayward friend?"

"Shoot, we've got plenty of space. And if you don't mind getting your hands dirty, I could sure use some help with this painting business."

And just like that, I had my summer plans sorted. Joe Fox, bless his heart, agreed to drop me off in Austin on his way to the clinic. The drive was long, but the conversation flowed easy as a lazy river.

As we pulled into Larry's driveway, I whistled low. "That's some house, alright."

Larry came bounding out, all six-foot-four of him, grinning like a possum eating sweet potatoes. He also had a swollen, black right eye.

First thing I said was, "What happened, Larry?"

Larry said, "I play for the town's baseball team as the catcher. A wild pitch knocked off my face cage and caught me in the right eye. Welcome to Casa Kramer, boys!"

After Joe headed off, Larry showed me to the guest room. "It ain't much, but it's home," he said, scratching the back of his neck.

"It's perfect," I assured him. "Now, about this painting job..."

Larry's face lit up like a Christmas tree. "Oh boy, you're in for a treat! Daddy's got us set up with enough paint to cover the whole dang town."

The next morning, we were up with the roosters. Larry's dad, a sturdy man with hands like baseball mitts, gave us our marching orders.

"Now boys," he drawled, "I want this house looking prettier than a speckled pup. You hear?"

Dad then headed off to work leaving us a fourteen-foot ladder and all the paint we could use.

"Yes sir," we chorused, trying not to laugh.

Days blurred together in a haze of white paint and country music blaring from an old radio. We'd work from sunup to sundown, trading stories, and jokes.

"Hey Larry," I called one afternoon, wiping sweat from my brow, "remember that time in Lincoln when you tried to impress that girl by doing a backflip off the bleachers?"

Larry groaned. "Don't remind me. I thought I was hot stuff until I landed flat on my keister."

We laughed so hard, sometimes we'd nearly fall off our ladders. Larry did not like height, so he had me up on the ladder doing the second-story painting.

Evenings were a different story. We'd clean up, put on our best white T-shirts, and hit the town. Austin might've been small, but it sure knew how to have a good time.

"C'mon," Larry would say, slapping me on the back. "Let's go see what kind of trouble we can get into."

We'd meet up with his high school buddies at the local diner, sharing baskets of fries and swapping tall tales.

"Remember when Larry here tried to ask out Sally Mae?" one of his friends, a redhead named Tommy, would start.

Larry would groan, "Not this story again."

But we'd all lean in, eager to hear how the big football star fumbled his words worse than a rookie quarterback.

As August rolled around, the house was looking mighty fine, and Larry was getting antsy about heading back to Lincoln for football camp.

"You gonna be alright?" he asked me one night as we sat on the porch, watching fireflies dance in the twilight.

I nodded, feeling a bit lost. "Reckon so. Might head back to Lincoln myself, see about picking up some work."

And that's just what I did. Come September, I was back in the hustle and bustle of city life, juggling more jobs than a circus performer.

My first gig was at the University Club, serving fancy folks their dinner. I'd clock out at 11:30, then hightail it over to the VFW club for my second shift.

Now, the VFW was a different animal altogether. It was what they called a "bottle club," staying open 'til the wee hours of the morning.

"Listen up, rookie," my manager, a gruff old veteran named Bill, told me on my first night. "Folks here bring their own liquor. Your job is to lock it up and serve it back to 'em, along with whatever mixer they want. Got it?"

I nodded, feeling like I was being let in on some big secret.

The club would come alive after midnight when the college kids showed up, full of energy and looking to dance.

"Hey barkeep!" they'd holler. "Set us up for some Mombo Rock!"

I'd watch, amazed, as they'd contort themselves, shimmying under a lowering bar without touching it. It was like a game of limbo, but with more hip-swinging and less tropical flair.

By the time I'd lock up and trudge home to my little basement apartment—courtesy of good ol' George Haney—the sun would peek over the horizon.

But there was no rest for the weary. I'd catch a few winks, then be up and at 'em by 8:00 a.m., pedaling my bike to my day job at the paper company.

"Morning, sunshine," my coworker, a burly fellow named Chuck, would greet me. "Ready to wrestle some paper rolls?"

And wrestle, we did. Those rolls weighed more than a prize hog at the county fair, but we'd muscle them off the truck and into the print shops all over Lincoln.

It was a grueling schedule, but I was determined to save up enough for tuition. Come January, I was back in class, chasing after that Physical Ed degree with a newfound appreciation for the value of hard work and good friends.

Looking back, that summer in Austin with Larry, and those long nights at the VFW, they taught me more about life than any textbook ever could. And you know what? I wouldn't have traded those experiences for all the tea in China.

Chapter 23: Peach State Shenanigans

Let me tell you about the time George Haney and I took a wild ride down to Atlanta, Georgia. It was Christmas vacation, and I'd cleared my schedule faster than a fox in a henhouse. The paper company job? Gone. The VFW club? Closed up tighter than a drum. Even sweet June Krueger at the University Club gave me her blessing for two weeks off.

George and I hit the road early, his old car chugging along like a tired mule. We'd been driving for what felt like days when we crossed into Arkansas. The sun had long since tipped its hat and said goodnight, and I was nodding off something fierce.

Suddenly, George's voice cut through the fog in my brain. "Jimmy, wake up! There's someone behind us that looks suspicious."

I rubbed my eyes, trying to focus. "What do you mean?"

George's knuckles were white on the steering wheel. "We've got Georgia plates on this car, and these hillbillies don't take kindly to southern boys. That car behind us has been playing cat and mouse for miles, flashing their lights on and off."

My heart started racing faster than a jackrabbit. "What should I do?"

"Reach under your seat," George said, his voice low and serious. "There's a crowbar down there. Bring it up here. If they stop us, you might need to start swinging."

I fumbled around and found the cold metal bar, my palms sweaty. George stomped on the gas, and we shot forward like a bullet from a gun. Those fellas behind us couldn't keep up, and after a spell, we lost 'em.

Hours later, with George about ready to keel over from driving, we pulled into a little town park. He shook me awake. "Jimmy, you get out and climb up on that picnic table. I need to lay down in the front seat."

I stumbled out, wrapping my topcoat around me like a cocoon. The night air was chillier than a stepmother's kiss. I must've dozed off because the next thing I knew, I woke up to the sun peeking over the horizon, and I was covered in a blanket of snow.

"George!" I called out, shivering like a leaf. "Fire up that heater before I turn into an icicle!"

We thawed out and made it to Atlanta by noon, pulling up to George's house like we'd just won the Indy 500.

A couple days before New Year's, I called my old friend Bill Childers. He was in Hickory, North Carolina, itching for a ride back to Lincoln.

"Come on down," I told him. "We'll make it a party." Afterward, I asked George, "Would it be all right for Billy to ride back to Nebraska with us?" George was fine with the idea.

Now, George's sister was a real peach. She rustled up a New Year's Eve shindig for us, even found a girl for Billy. That evening, we piled into her mama's car. She drove us downtown to this big hall that had a live band.

Billy, sly as a fox, says to me, "I used to live here, you know. Got some friends nearby having a party. Mind if I give 'em a call?"

While he was yakking on the phone, George's sister and her friend decided they'd had enough. "We're heading home, boys," she said, handing me the car keys. "Y'all be careful now."

Billy's eyes lit up like fireworks. "Jim, my buddy's place is just three blocks from here. What say we walk on over?"

I patted my coat pocket, feeling the familiar shape of a bottle. "I've still got some Canadian Club. All we need is some 7-Up."

We moseyed over to Billy's friend's place, where the party was in full swing. "Make yourselves at home, boys!" our host hollered over the music.

We found our 7-Up and mixed up a few drinks. A while later, it was high time we headed back to George's house. The sun was just rising, and the party became very quiet.

Now, here's where things got interesting. We stumbled back to the car, and I turned to Billy. "You know how to get back to George's?"

Billy scratched his head. "Uh, sorta?"

I fired up the engine and pulled onto the first interstate I saw. "I reckon we just take this freeway for a spell," I said, squinting at the road signs.

We cruised along, watching for anything that looked familiar. Finally, a street name caught my eye. "That sounds about right," I said, taking the exit.

As we wound our way through the neighborhood, things started looking less and less familiar. "Billy," I said, a sinking feeling in my gut, "We might be lost."

Billy leaned forward, peering out the windshield. "Nah, it's gotta be around here somewhere. Maybe take a left up there?"

We turned down one street after another, each looking less like George's neighborhood than the last. The houses started getting bigger, fancier.

"Jim," Billy said, his voice suddenly serious, "We might be in the governor's mansion neighborhood."

Just then, we saw flashing lights in the rearview mirror. A police car was pulling us over.

"Oh, lord," I muttered, easing the car to the curb.

The officer sauntered up to our window, shining his flashlight in our faces. "Evening, gentlemen. Seems like you boys are a long way from home."

I tried my best to explain our situation, but I reckon our breath gave us away. The officer's mustache twitched. "Step out of the car, please."

Chapter 24: My Unexpected Stay in the Atlanta Slammer

Now, I ain't proud of what I did next, but desperation makes fools of us all. I fished out my library card, hoping the picture and name might tell the officer my identification.

"Billy," I hissed, "hand me your driver's license, quick!"

Billy's eyes went wide as saucers. "I can't give you my license!"

Before I could argue, we heard a tap on the window that sounded like judgment day coming. I rolled it down, plastering on my best "aw shucks" smile.

"Evening, officer," I said, handing over my library card. "Seems I've left my license at home."

The officer's eyes narrowed. "Step out of the car, son."

As I stumbled out, he hit me with the million-dollar question: "How many drinks have you had tonight?"

Now, I've never been one for lying, but I sure wasn't about to tell the whole truth. "Oh, maybe two or three," I said, trying to sound casual.

Next thing I knew, I was sitting in the back of the patrol car, watching the officer chat with Billy in the front of the patrol car. That's when I had what I thought was a stroke of genius. I rolled down the back window, quiet as a church mouse, I pulled out that half-pint of Canadian Club that had been burning a hole in my pocket all night. I spotted a patch of grass between the curb and sidewalk. "Perfect," I thought. "I'll just toss the bottle there, nice and quiet-like."

Well, let me tell you, things rarely go as planned when you're three sheets to the wind. That bottle hit the grass alright, but then it slid right onto the sidewalk and shattered louder than my grandma's best china hitting a tile floor.

Before I knew it, I was standing in front of a cage window at the police station, emptying my pockets into a plastic bag like I was checking into some twisted hotel. They took my picture holding a sign with numbers, and I felt like I was starring in my episode of "America's Dumbest Criminals."

The jail keeper, a burly fella with a face like a bulldog chewing a wasp, led me to a cell. "You'll be safe in here for the night," he growled, removing my handcuffs.

I collapsed onto the bunk and passed out faster than a lightweight at a frat party. When I woke up, sunlight was streaming through the barred window, and the drunk tank sound down the hall was making more noise than a henhouse full of foxes.

The next day, the turnkey, about the same age as myself, came to my cell. He was a chatty sort, asking me all kinds of questions. "Where you from, son? Got family here in Atlanta? How are you planning on getting back to Nebraska?"

Then he offered me a reprieve from my cell. "How'd you like to come up front for a spell?"

I followed him like a puppy, hands clasped behind my back, still wearing my rumpled green corduroy suit minus the tie.

In the visitor's room that morning, I found George Haney waiting for me, looking as uncomfortable as a long-tailed cat in a room full of rocking chairs.

"Jimmy," he said, "Billy and I gotta head back to Lincoln today. Classes start next week. You got any money?"

I shook my head. "About eight bucks downstairs. I don't have a pot to piss in or a window to throw it out of." George then asked, "Do you have any relatives who can help you get out of here? My answer was, "I don't have any relative that I can get a hold of because they don't have my little black book."

George sighed, then brightened up. "I've got a buddy who works downstairs. Name's Leroy. When you check out, ask for him. But

Jimmy," he paused, looking grim, "courts are closed till Tuesday 'cause of the holiday. You're gonna be in here five days before you see a judge."

My stomach dropped like an elevator with cut cables. "I understand, George. You and Billy get on back to Lincoln. And tell your mama I'm sorry about the dent in her car. Swear on my life, we didn't do that."

After George left, I was back in my cell. I stripped down to my skivvies to keep my suit neat. I found a small tablet and pen in my jacket pocket and set about making my own deck of cards. Figured I'd need something to keep me busy during my extended stay.

The food was something else. When the turnkey brought my first meal, I thought he was playing a joke. Fried pig fat they called "chic lets," hominy grits, and some boiled green leaves that looked like a tractor had run over them.

"This what y'all consider food 'round here?" I asked, poking at the grits with my fork.

The turnkey just grinned. "Welcome to the South, son. Eat up. It's good for ya."

As I sat there, playing solitaire with my homemade cards and choking down what passed for meals, I had plenty of time to reflect on my poor life choices. I thought about Aunt Ella back home, how disappointed she'd be if she knew where I was. I thought about my classes starting without me, and about the opportunities I might be missing.

I thought about how I was gonna explain this whole mess when I finally got out. 'Cause one thing was for sure—this wasn't a story I'd be bragging about anytime soon.

As the days crawled by slower than molasses in January, I made a promise to myself. If I ever got out of this jam, I was gonna straighten up and fly right. No more wild nights, no more riding in cars with boys who couldn't find their way home.

Little did I know, my adventure in the Atlanta city jail was far from over. But that, my friends, is a story for another day.

Chapter 25: The Nebraska Kid's Wild Ride

Well, folks, let me tell you about the day I became the star attraction of the Atlanta city jail. On my second day behind bars, and I thought I might grow roots in that cell.

The turnkey, a fella who took a liking to me as a friend, had a face that looked younger than me. He came by early the third morning.

"How'd you like to come out and sit with me for a spell?" he asked, jingling his keys like they were Christmas bells.

I perked up faster than a dog hearing a dinner bell. "Beats sitting in this cell all day!"

The door creaked open, and I followed him like a lost puppy to his little station. He had himself a steel chair fit for a king, while I got a stool that looked like it might collapse if I sneezed wrong.

"What do you think about all day in that cell?" he asked, eyeing me curiously.

I chuckled, "Well, sir, I've become quite the card shark. Made myself a deck and been playing solitaire till my fingers are raw."

He nodded, impressed. "Where you from, son?"

"Nebraska," I said, puffing up a bit with pride. "I'm a student at the university there. Or at least I was before this little...vacation."

The turnkey's eyes twinkled with mischief. "Say, where's your fancy duds? You didn't wear that T-shirt to your New Year's shindig, did you?"

I explained about me taking my suit and white shirt and placing them on the bunk bed above my bed to keep the clothing neat, and that's when he got this idea that would change the course of my day.

"Mind if I call you the 'Nebraska Kid?'" he asked, grinning like a possum eating sweet potatoes. "Got some Cub Scouts coming through later this afternoon. Thought we might have some fun."

Before I could answer, a ruckus broke out down in the drunk tank. Sounded like a bar brawl had spilled over into jail. The turnkey hustled me back to my cell and went to sort out the commotion.

After a lunch that could be called a ham sandwich (if you squinted real hard), the turnkey came back. "Put on your jacket, Nebraska Kid. The scouts are coming."

I slipped on my green corduroy jacket, feeling like I was getting dressed up for the strangest party of my life.

Soon enough, I heard the pitter-patter of little feet and excited whispers. The turnkey's voice boomed down the hall, "And here, boys, we have a very special prisoner. This here's the Nebraska Kid. Take a good look at him. Does he look like he belongs in jail?"

Now, I don't know what came over me, but suddenly I was overcome with the urge to put on a show. I leaped up, grabbed the cell bars, and let out a growl that would've made a grizzly bear proud. Those bars rattled like they were escaping themselves.

You should've seen those Cub Scouts! They jumped back so fast; you'd think the floor was on fire. A couple of them let out yelps that could've woken the dead.

The turnkey, bless his heart, played along. "See, boys? Mean and ugly, ain't he? That's why he's locked up tight!"

After the tour moved on, the turnkey came back, chuckling. "Jim, my boy, that was a performance. How'd you like to do an encore? We've got a lineup later if you're up for it."

Well, I was so starved for entertainment, I would've volunteered to wrestle a bear if he'd asked. "Count me in!" I said, grinning from ear to ear.

Come four o'clock, the turnkey led me down to a room with a big mirror on one wall. I knew enough about cop shows to figure it was one of them two-way mirrors.

"Stand on that number one spot," he instructed, "and face the mirror."

Six other fellas filed in behind me, lining up like ducks in a row. They handed us cards to hold under our chins, like some twisted version of a school picture day.

The turnkey had us turn this way and that, like we were modeling the latest in-prison fashion. Then came the kicker.

"Number one," he called out, "step forward and state your full name."

For a split second, I panicked. Was this a real lineup? Did I look like some other ne'er-do-well? But I squared my shoulders and gave it my best shot.

"James William Brown," I declared, trying to sound as innocent as a newborn babe.

After we'd all had our turn in the spotlight, the turnkey dismissed the others and pulled me aside.

"Jim," he said, his voice turning serious, "tomorrow's your day in court."

My stomach did a somersault that would've made an Olympic gymnast proud.

"Now listen close," he continued. "In the morning, put on that fancy coat and shirt of yours. Button it up tight, right to the top. They'll come to get you, and they'll put cuffs on your ankles and wrists."

I must've looked as green as my corduroy jacket because he clapped me on the shoulder. "Keep your chin up, son. And try to keep a smile on your face. I'm off duty tomorrow morning, but I'll be rooting for you."

As I rested in my bunk that night, staring at the ceiling and listening to the snores and mutters of my fellow inmates, I wondered what tomorrow would bring. Would I head home to Nebraska, tail between my legs? Or was I in for a longer stay in the Atlanta Hilton, as I'd started calling it?

One thing was for sure—this wasn't how I'd planned to start my new year. But as George Haney always said, "Life's what happens when you're busy making other plans." And boy, had life happened to me.

I closed my eyes, said a sincere prayer, and dreamed of wide-open Nebraska skies. Tomorrow was another day, and whatever it brought, I'd face it head-on. After all, I was the Nebraska Kid now. I had a reputation to uphold.

Chapter 26: Judgment Day

Well, folks, the day of reckoning had finally arrived. I woke up that morning feeling like a turkey on Thanksgiving Day. My stomach was doing more flips than a circus acrobat as I buttoned up my shirt and slipped on that green corduroy jacket.

Breakfast was a hunk of beef jerky that could've passed for shoe leather. As I gnawed on it, the cell door creaked open. Two guards stood there, looking about as friendly as a pair of rattlesnakes.

"Time to go, Nebraska Kid," one of them drawled.

Before I knew it, I was trussed up tighter than a Christmas turkey with cuffs on my wrists, and chains jangling down to shackles on my ankles. I had to shuffle along like a penguin with a bad case of frostbite.

They herded me and four other poor souls onto an elevator. We were packed in tighter than sardines in a can, with four beefy policemen for company. The ride down was quieter than a library on a Sunday morning.

As the elevator doors opened, I half expected to see the Pearly Gates. Instead, we were met by a van that looked like it had seen better days. We clambered in, settling onto benches that felt about as comfortable as sitting on a pile of rocks.

As we rattled along toward the courthouse, my mind raced faster than a greyhound chasing a mechanical rabbit.

"This is it," I thought. "I'm headed for the Georgia chain gang. Goodbye, Nebraska. Goodbye, college. Hello, life of breaking rocks and singing "Swing Low, Sweet Chariot."

When we arrived at the courthouse, I felt so nervous I nearly face-planted getting out of the van. Thankfully, one of the guards caught me before I could add "eating concrete" to my list of crimes.

They marched us into the courtroom and sat us down on a bench in front of the judge's stand. Let me tell you, that judge was perched up so high, you'd think he was trying to touch the clouds. To look at him, you had to crane your neck like you were watching a fireworks show.

The first fella they called up was named King. Turns out, he was a frequent flyer in these parts.

The judge's voice boomed out like thunder. "Mr. King, my records tell me this is your third time darkening my doorstep in two years. That correct?"

King mumbled something that wouldn't have woken a sleeping mouse.

"Speak up, son!" the judge bellowed. "I can't hear you over the sound of your poor life choices!"

Poor old King ended up with thirty-three weeks on the chain gang. The sound of that gavel coming down was like a nail in my coffin.

Next up was Williams, a little fella sitting next to me. Turns out, he'd been caught driving drunk...again.

"Sir," Williams pleaded, "I only drove five blocks before I saw the flashing lights. I swear, I'll never do it again!"

The judge wasn't buying it. "You won't be doing it for six months, that's for sure. Chain gang for you, Mr. Williams."

By this point, I was shaking like a leaf in a hurricane. When they called my name, I stood up so fast I nearly toppled over. My knees knocked together like castanets.

As I shuffled to the front, the judge peered down at me like I was some kind of peculiar bug.

"Mr. James Brown," he intoned, "you're here on charges of drunk driving. That correct?"

"Yes, sir!" I squeaked, trying to sound confident but coming off more like a mouse with a head cold.

The judge squinted at me. "Spread your feet apart, son. You look like you're about to keel over."

I did as I was told, feeling about as steady as a newborn colt.

Then, out of nowhere, the judge hit me with a curveball. "How can you be in jail for five days and not have even a hint of stubble?"

I blinked, caught off guard. "Well, sir," I stammered, "I only have to shave once or twice a month on account of my peach fuzz."

A ghost of a smile flickered across the judge's face. "And your shirt...do they iron clothes in jail now? It's hardly wrinkled!"

"No, sir," I explained, feeling a bit proud of myself. "First night in my cell, I took off my shirt and coat and put them on the top bunk to keep 'em neat."

The judge's eyebrows shot up. "Well, I'll be. Most of my...clients...can't think that far ahead. Where did you say you were from, Mr. Brown?"

"Nebraska, sir," I replied, standing a little straighter.

The judge leaned back, stroking his chin. "Mr. Brown, I'm going to sentence you to probation. Do you know what that means?"

I shook my head, hope starting to bubble up inside me like a freshly opened soda.

"It means," he explained, "that if I see your face in my courtroom again in the next two years, you'll be swapping that fancy jacket for a set of stripes. You understand?"

"Yes, sir!" I nearly shouted, relief washing over me like a tidal wave.

The judge's gavel came down with a bang that echoed through my very soul. But this time, it was the sweetest sound I'd ever heard.

As they led me out of the courtroom, I felt like I was walking on air. No chain gang for this Nebraska kid. I was going home, back to wide open skies and the promise of a fresh start.

Right then and there, I made a solemn vow. No more wild nights, no more joyriding, and no more flirting with disaster. From now on, I would be straighter than an arrow and cleaner than a whistle.

As I stepped into the Georgia sunshine, a free man once more, I couldn't help but grin. I'd dodged a bullet, no doubt about it. And let me tell you, folks, this was one lesson I wasn't about to forget anytime soon.

The Nebraska Kid was heading home, a little older, a little wiser, and a whole lot more appreciative of the simple things in life—like not wearing chains and walking without shuffling. It was time to get back to school, hit the books, and make something of myself.

After all, I had a promise to keep—to myself, to that judge, and to the good folks back home in Nebraska. And this time, I wouldn't let anyone down.

Chapter 27: Free as a Bird, Broke as a Joke

Well, there I was, finally free as a bird but broker than a church mouse on Sunday. The sun was shining brighter than a new penny, and the fresh air felt sweeter than store bought apple pie. But I had about as much direction as a tumbleweed in a tornado.

As I shuffled out of that jailhouse, a guard grabbed my arm. "Follow me, kid," he growled, leading me down the hall to a room with a counter protected by more wire than a chicken coop.

The fella behind the desk, Leroy, turned out to be a friend of George Haney's. He handed me a plastic bag with my worldly possessions—all eight dollars and sixty-three cents of it.

"Listen up, Jim," Leroy said, leaning in close. "When you get out, turn right, go to the corner, then left. Look for a sign that says 'Bail Bondsman' in yellow letters brighter than a canary. Ask for Al and tell him Leroy sent you. He'll take care of you."

I nodded, feeling like I'd just been given the secret map to buried treasure.

As I stepped out into the Atlanta sunshine, I felt like a newborn colt—wobbly, confused, but darn excited to be alive. I followed Leroy's directions like they were the word of God Himself, and soon enough, I was face-to-face with Al, the bail bondsman.

Al was on the phone when I arrived, so I sat there fidgeting like a long-tailed cat in a room full of rocking chairs. When he finally hung up, he turned to me with a look that was part curiosity, part pity.

"So, kid," he drawled, "you got a place to stay in Atlanta?"

I shook my head, feeling about as useful as a screen door on a submarine.

"Any money?"

I emptied my pockets onto his desk—all eight dollars of my fortune.

Al whistled low. "Son, you couldn't get out of sight on a cloudy day with that cash. You got anyone who can lend you some money?"

I shook my head again, feeling lower than a snake's belly in a wagon rut.

But Al, bless his heart, wasn't about to let this lost Nebraska boy flounder. "Alright, here's what we're gonna do," he said, leaning forward. "I've got a bed in the back room and a bathroom you can use. We'll get you a toothbrush and some toiletries. Tomorrow, we'll see about getting you home."

I could've hugged that man right then and there, but I settled for a heartfelt, "Thank you, sir."

That night, I slept like a baby on that mattress. After a week of jail bunks, it felt like sleeping on a cloud. The next morning, Al took me on a collection run. I felt like I was in one of those gangster movies, but Al assured me it was all above board.

When we got back, Al called up the Travelers Aid Society and set me up with an appointment. He sent me off with directions and a pep talk that would've made a football coach proud.

I put on my green corduroy suit, slicked back my hair, and headed out feeling like a million bucks—even if my pockets were emptier than a politician's promises.

The Travelers Aid office was locked up tighter than Fort Knox when I got there, but a man eventually let me in. He listened to my sob story with a sympathetic ear, but when he was done, he looked at me like I'd just asked him to lasso the moon.

"Son," he said, shaking his head, "you've picked a bad time to need help. We're fresh out of funds after the holiday season."

My heart sank faster than a lead balloon. But then, miracle of miracles, he reached into his own wallet and pulled out a crisp ten-dollar bill.

"It ain't much," he said, "but it might keep you fed for a day or two while you figure things out."

I thanked him like he'd just handed me the keys to the city and headed back to Al's office. On the way, I spotted the Greyhound station. I walked into the station and asked what it would cost to take a bus from Atlanta to Lincoln, Nebraska.

The lady at the counter punched some numbers into her adding machine and looked at me with pity. "Seventy dollars to Lincoln, Nebraska," she said.

I felt like I'd been punched in the gut. Seventy dollars might as well have been a million.

When I got back to Al's and told him the news, he scratched his chin thoughtfully. "Jim," he said, "you got any friends back in Nebraska who might be able to pass the hat around? Seventy for the ticket, plus some eating money—you're looking at needing about ninety dollars."

I wracked my brain, trying to think of anyone who might be able to help. It was a long shot, but it was the only shot I had.

"There might be a few folks," I said, hope rising in my chest like a bubble. "Can I use your phone, Mr. Al?"

Al nodded, pushing the phone toward me. "Have at it, kid. And call me Al. After all we've been through, we're practically family now."

As I picked up that phone, my hand shaking like a leaf in a thunderstorm, I sent up a silent prayer. "Lord," I thought, "if you're listening, now would be a real good time for a miracle. This Nebraska kid needs to get home."

I took a deep breath and started dialing. It was time to see if I had any friends left in this world. One thing was for sure—if I ever made it back to Nebraska, I was never going to take home for granted again. Atlanta had been one heck of an adventure, but this cowboy was ready to ride off into the sunset—if only I could rustle up the cash for a bus ticket.

Chapter 28: Passing the Hat

Well, folks, there I was, stuck in Atlanta with nothing but lint in my pockets and a prayer on my lips. But as my grandpappy used to say, "When you're at the end of your rope, tie a knot and hang on." So that's just what I did.

I dug out my little black book—and let me tell you, that thing was more valuable than gold right about then. I found the number for the training room back at the university and gave ol' George Sullivan a ring.

"George," I said, sounding calmer than a cucumber, "I need you to get a message to Steve Olson. Tell him to call me at this number. I'm in a bit of a pickle down here in Atlanta."

About an hour later, that phone rang like Gabriel's trumpet. It was Steve Olson, bless his heart.

"Jim?" he said, sounding like he couldn't believe his ears. "I hear you're in Atlanta. Did you really end up in the slammer?"

I chuckled, though it wasn't really funny. "Sure did, Steve. But I'm out now. Thing is, I'm about as broke as the Ten Commandments. I need about ninety bucks to get home. You think you could pass the hat around for me?"

Steve, good ol' Steve, didn't even hesitate. "I'll see what I can do, buddy. But I'll need an address to send the money to."

I gave him Al's address, feeling a glimmer of hope for the first time in days.

The next day, Steve called back. "Jim, I'm working on it. Trying to get hold of Gary Ward from Fremont—you know he's always flush. And I've put in a call to Dave Cook, that wrestler from Jersey."

I crossed my fingers so hard I thought they might break.

Another day passed, and I was pacing Al's office like a caged tiger when the phone rang again.

"Jim!" Steve's voice was excited. "We did it! We raised enough to get you home. I'm sending it Western Union this afternoon."

I nearly whooped loud enough to wake the dead. "Steve, you're a lifesaver. I owe you big time."

That afternoon, a Western Union fella showed up with a money order for $85. I felt like I'd just won the lottery.

I scrounged up a paper bag, tossed in my toothbrush and toothpaste, and stuffed it in my corduroy suit pocket. Al, bless his heart, took me to the bank to cash the check, then drove me to the Greyhound station.

"Go on in and see when the next bus to Lincoln leaves," Al said, a twinkle in his eye.

I turned to him, feeling a lump in my throat the size of a golf ball. "Al," I said, looking him square in the eye, "thank you. For everything. You're gonna go to heaven for this, I just know it. And I bet your clients won't give you half as much trouble from now on."

Al just smiled and patted me on the back. "Get on home, kid. And stay out of trouble, will ya?"

As I walked into that bus station, I felt like a new man. I may have come to Atlanta with stars in my eyes, but I was leaving with a whole lot more—a renewed appreciation for home, some hard-earned wisdom, and the knowledge that even when things look darkest, there are good people in this world willing to lend a helping hand.

The Nebraska Kid was heading home, a little older, a little wiser, and a lot more grateful. Atlanta had been one heck of an adventure, but I was ready for the wide-open skies of Nebraska. As I bought my ticket, I couldn't help but grin. This was one trip I'd be telling stories about for years to come.

Chapter 29: From Jailbird to the Governor's Guest

Well, folks, let me tell you about the most interesting bus ride of my life. It was a journey that took me from the back of a police van to the lap of luxury, with a whole lot of life lessons in between.

That bus ride back to Lincoln? It felt longer than a month of Sundays. Two and a half days, to be exact. And there I was, still wearing that green corduroy suit that had seen better days. It was starting to look about as wrinkled as a prune and probably smelled worse.

I started out sitting pretty, right up front by the driver. I figured I'd get a good view of America rolling by, and maybe strike up a conversation with the fella behind the wheel. But let me tell you, after two days and two nights on that bus, I was riper than a week-old banana left out in the sun.

Somewhere in Kansas City, the driver, a burly fella with a mustache that could've doubled as a push broom, cleared his throat and said, "Uh, Mr. Brown? Would you mind moving to the back of the bus? It's getting a little...fragrant up here in the front."

I could've died of embarrassment right then and there. But I just nodded, gathered what was left of my dignity, and shuffled to the back where the black folks were sitting. They welcomed me with knowing smiles and sympathetic nods. One old gentleman even offered me a stick of gum, bless his heart.

From Kansas City, I scrounged up enough change to give Steve Olson a call.

"Steve," I said, trying not to sound as desperate as I felt, "I'm on my way home. Any chance you could meet me at the bus depot?"

"Sure thing, Brownie," Steve replied. "Gary Warden and I will be there. Don't you worry."

When that bus finally pulled into Lincoln, I felt like kissing the ground. There was Gary, waiting for me with a grin wider than the Platte River.

"Follow me, Brownie," he said, clapping me on the back. "We've got a chariot waiting for you."

Outside, I was introduced to our driver, a clean-cut fella named Johnny Morrison. Little did I know, I was about to go from rags to riches in the blink of an eye.

We headed straight for the DB&G, the local watering hole where all the college kids hung out. Johnny ordered a pitcher of red beer and three glasses, and we settled in for some serious catching up.

As we were sipping our beers, Johnny leaned in and said, "Jim, you're coming home with me tonight. You need a good bath and a proper rest."

Now, I was so grateful I could've hugged the man right then and there. But it wasn't until we pulled up to a house that looked like it belonged in a movie that I realized just who Johnny Morrison was.

"Welcome to the governor's mansion," Johnny said with a wink.

My jaw nearly hit the floor. "Governor's mansion?" I stuttered.

Johnny just laughed. "That's right. My old man's the governor. Hope you don't mind bunking with political royalty for the night."

I slept like a baby that night, cleaner than I'd been in weeks, and tucked into sheets softer than a cloud. The next morning, as I made my way back to the dorm, still in a daze from my brush with high society, Steve Olson met me with a grin.

"Brownie," he said, shaking his head in disbelief, "you're the only guy I've ever known to go from the jailhouse to the governor's mansion in one fell swoop. You sure know how to make an entrance...and an exit!"

I couldn't help but laugh. It had been one heck of a journey, that was for sure. As I settled into my classes, trying to make up for those lost two weeks, I reflected on the wild ride I'd been on.

From the highs of New Year's Eve in Atlanta to the lows of a jail cell, from the kindness of strangers like Al the bail bondsman to the loyalty of friends like Steve and Gary, and from the back of a Greyhound bus to the governor's guest room—it had been an adventure I'd never forget.

And as I cracked open my textbooks, ready to dive into the world of academia, I thought maybe, just maybe, I'd learned more in those two crazy weeks than I ever could in a classroom. Life has a funny way of teaching its lessons, and boy, had I gotten an education.

But one thing was for sure—it was good to be home. The Nebraska Kid was back where he belonged, with stories to tell and a newfound appreciation for the simple things in life—like clean clothes, good friends, and the ability to walk more than ten feet without chains on your ankles.

Chapter 30: Thumbs Out

It was my senior year at college, and I swear, either the classes were getting easier, or I was getting smarter. I'd gone back to working as a bartender at the University Club, studying at night and closing up shop around 11:00 p.m.

During spring break, my buddy Billy Childers sauntered up to me with a gleam in his eye. "Hey Jim," he says, "how 'bout you and I hitchhike down to see my mama in Hickory, North Carolina?"

I scratched my head. "Hitchhike? All the way to North Carolina? You sure about that, Billy?"

"Sure as shooting," he grins. "It'll be an adventure!"

"Well, alright," I said, "but what do I need to pack?"

Billy chuckled. "Not much, partner. A pair of jeans, couple shirts, some undies, and a few clean socks. We're traveling light—just one suitcase between us."

So, on Friday, after our last class, a friend dropped us off south of Lincoln. There we were, two college boys standing on the side of the highway, thumbs out, hoping for the best.

The third car that passed us pulled over. The driver leaned out, asking, "Where you boys headed?"

"Hickory, North Carolina, sir," Billy said, all polite-like.

"Well, I can get you as far as Beatrice," the driver offered.

We hop in, grateful for the ride. In Beatrice, we ducked into a filling station to study a map.

"Looks like we oughta head to Marysville," I say, "then take Highway 36 to St. Joseph's."

Lady Luck was smiling on us 'cause a salesman picked us up next. "Where you fellas going?" he asks.

We tell him our plan, and he shakes his head. "Nah, you want to stay on 36 to Hamilton, then take 13 down to Interstate 70. Bypasses Kansas City and shoots you straight to St. Louis."

He drops us off in Stewartville, and we follow his advice. By 4:30, we're on I-70, thumbs out again. An old fella gives us a fifty-mile ride before dropping us off in the middle of nowhere.

Now, I-70's a fast road. Trucks and cars whizzing by, and no one wants to stop. We start walking, but as the sun goes down, so does the temperature.

"Billy," I say, teeth chattering, "we gotta find some shelter."

We spot a bridge and hunker down underneath. "Let's try to start a fire," Billy suggests.

We scrounge up some dead grass and weeds, and I pull out my little black book with a pack of matches. The fire's pitiful, barely warming our hands, but it's something.

As the night wears on, the cold seeps into our bones. We layer on extra jeans from the suitcase, but sleep's impossible with all of them trucks rumbling overhead.

"This ain't working," Billy groans. "Might as well keep walking."

So we trudge along in the dark, our thumbs out more outta habit than hope. After what feels like forever, we see a sign: "Columbia 35 miles."

Just as the sun's peeking over the horizon, a car finally pulls over. The driver looks rough, with bloodshot eyes and a twitchy demeanor.

"Hop in," he says. "Maybe you can help me drive."

We pile in, and he floors it, the speedometer nudging seventy.

"Been driving two days straight from California," he explains. "Gotta get to New York for my grandma's funeral."

He reaches under the seat and pulls out a bag. "Want some of these? Keep you awake."

Billy eyes the pills suspiciously. "What are they?"

"Bennies," the driver says. "I got two more days of driving. Gotta stay alert."

"No thanks," Billy says firmly. "We're just trying to get to St. Louis."

The driver shrugs. "Suit yourself. Either of you want to drive?"

Billy volunteers, and soon our twitchy friend is snoring in the backseat. We make it through St. Louis and switch back near I-65.

Our next ride comes quick—a fella named Mr. Steele. He's heading to Louisville and seems mighty interested in our story.

"You boys need a sign," he advises. "Folk are more likely to pick you up if they know where you're going."

We stop for gas in a little town called Vernon, and Mr. Steele offers to buy us breakfast. "There's a Five & Dime across the street," he says. "Go get some poster board and a marker. I'll meet you at the diner next door."

As we're picking out supplies, I nudge Billy. "Why's he being so nice? What's his angle?"

Billy shrugs. "Maybe he's just a good guy. But keep your guard up, just in case."

Over breakfast, Mr. Steele peppers us with questions and talks about his work as a clothing and shoe salesman.

"You know," he says, wiping his mouth, "I got a brother in Asheville. Ain't seen him in three years. It ain't too far from Hickory. What say I take you boys the rest of the way?"

He excuses himself to make a call, and when he comes back, he's all smiles. "My brother's tickled pink I'm coming to visit. You boys ready to hit the road?"

As we climb into his car, poster board in hand, I marvel at our luck. From shivering under a bridge to riding in style with Mr. Steele. It's been one heck of a journey.

"You know, Billy," I say as we pull onto the highway, "I reckon this hitchhiking idea of yours wasn't half bad after all."

Billy grins and pats the sign we made. "Just wait 'til we get to Hickory. Mama's gonna have a fit when she hears about our adventure!"

And with that, we settle in for the last leg of our trip, the open road stretched out before us, full of promise and possibility.

Chapter 31: Riding the Kindness Highway

We piled into Mr. Steele's car, our bellies full and spirits high. The man was a regular guardian angel, I tell you. As we cruised toward Louisville, he regaled us with tales of his travel salesman days.

"You boys ever been to Louisville?" Mr. Steele asked, his eyes twinkling.

Billy shook his head. "No sir, can't say we have."

"Well," Mr. Steele chuckled, "you're in for a treat. I know just the place for lunch."

True to his word, Mr. Steele treated us to a mighty fine meal in Louisville. The man seemed to take a shine to us, and I felt grateful for his kindness.

As evening rolled around and we pulled into Lexington, Kentucky, Mr. Steele turned to us with a smile. "Boys, what say we call it a night? I'll get us some rooms, and we can hit the road bright and early tomorrow."

Now, I ain't one to look a gift horse in the mouth, so Billy and I graciously accepted. Mr. Steele got himself a room, and we bunked down in another. As I lay there that night, I marveled at our luck.

"Billy," I whispered in the dark, "you reckon all folks are as kind as Mr. Steele?"

Billy yawned. "I dunno, Jim, but I sure am grateful we ran into him."

Come morning, Mr. Steele was true to his word. We were on the road by 6:30, after another breakfast on his dime. The man was generosity personified; I tell you.

When we reached Asheville, Mr. Steele pulled over on US 40. "Well, boys," he said, "this is where we part ways. Hickory's just up the road a piece."

We thanked him profusely, and I made sure to jot down his contact info in my trusty little black book. As we watched him drive away, I turned to Billy.

"You know, your crazy idea might just have restored my faith in humanity."

Billy grinned and held up our sign. "Let's see if our luck holds out."

Sure enough, the very first car that passed us screeched to a halt. The driver leaned out, a friendly face under a worn baseball cap. "Y'all headed to Hickory?"

"Yes sir," Billy replied, hardly believing our good fortune.

"Well, hop in!" the man said. "I'm headed that way myself. Where 'bouts in Hickory you boys going?"

When Billy gave him his mama's address, the driver's face lit up. "Why, I know that street! It's right on my way home. Ain't that something?"

As we pulled up to Billy's mama's house, I felt like we'd been touched by some kind of hitchhiker's magic. Billy's mama came bustling out, all smiles and happy tears.

"Oh, my sweet boy!" she cried, pulling Billy into a bear hug. "And you must be Jim! Come in, come in! I've got lunch all ready."

Billy's mama was a force of nature, I tell you. She had us settled at the table with plates piled high before we could even catch our breath. And boy, did she have questions! She wanted to know everything about Billy's life with his FBI brother, our classes, our trip—you name it.

As we ate, I noticed an old lady shuffling around the house, clutching a small can labeled "green peas." She must've been pushing ninety-five if she was a day.

Later, when Billy and I stepped out to visit his girlfriend, Hannah Laura, I had to ask. "Billy, what's the deal with the old lady and her can of peas?"

Billy burst out laughing. "Jim, my friend, that ain't no can of peas. That there's Mabel's spit can. She chews tobacco all day long!"

I nearly fell over laughing. Here I was, thinking it was some quirky old lady thing, and it turns out she was packing a lip the whole time!

We spent three fine days in Hickory, with Billy and Hannah Laura making googly eyes at each other the whole time. When it came time to leave, Billy's mama outdid herself. She handed us a brown paper sack bulging with goodies—ham and cheese sandwiches on little hamburger buns, and honest-to-goodness glass bottles of Coca-Cola.

"Now you boys be careful," she fussed, straightening Billy's collar. "And don't you dare lose my Tupperware!"

Hannah Laura drove us back to Asheville, and we hit I-40 with our sign flipped to "Lincoln, Nebraska." Lady Luck was still with us, because another salesman scooped us up and took us all the way to Knoxville.

In Knoxville, we had ourselves a little adventure on the city bus. Billy asked the driver how to get through town to I-40, and the kind soul told us to just stay put.

"This here bus'll take you right to the other side of town," he said with a wink.

So there we were, two college boys from Nebraska, munching on ham sandwiches and sipping Coke on a Knoxville city bus. When the driver dropped us off, he pointed us toward I-40.

"Just two blocks thataway, boys. Safe travels!"

Our next ride was something else entirely. A big old truck pulled over, but it wasn't any ordinary truck—it had another truck piggybacked on top! The driver, a burly fella with a handlebar mustache, explained he was delivering a truck chassis to Nashville.

As we climbed up into the cab, I felt like we were on top of the world. Billy pulled out our trusty snack sack, and we shared our bounty with our new friend.

"Well, I'll be," the driver said, biting into a sandwich. "You boys sure know how to travel in style!"

We rolled into Nashville around 6 o'clock, our heads full of truck stories and our hearts full of gratitude. As we checked into a downtown hotel for the night, I turned to Billy.

"You know," I said, "I reckon this trip's taught me something."

"Yeah?" Billy raised an eyebrow. "What's that?"

I grinned. "The world's full of good folks, just waiting for a chance to lend a hand. All you gotta do is stick out your thumb and trust in the kindness of strangers."

Billy nodded, a thoughtful look on his face.

"Amen to that, brother. Amen to that."

Chapter 32: Nashville Nights and Homeward Bound

We settled into our Nashville hotel room, but be young bucks full of vim and vigor, we weren't about to call it a night just yet.

"Say, Billy," I said, "how about we paint the town red?"

Billy grinned. "Now you're talking, Jim! Let's see what kind of trouble we can rustle up in Music City."

We moseyed on down to a nearby bar, feeling mighty thirsty. "Two 7 and 7s, if you please," I said to the bartender, trying to sound all sophisticated.

The bartender just chuckled. "Sorry, boys, but that ain't how we do things 'round here in Tennessee."

We must've looked as confused as a couple of cows on astroturf, 'cause he took pity on us and explained, "Y'all gotta go to the state liquor store two blocks down. Buy your hooch there, bring it back, and I'll sell you the mixer."

Well, I'll be darned if that wasn't the strangest thing I'd ever heard. But when in Rome, as they say. So off we trotted to the liquor store, came back with a half-pint of Seagram's 7 tucked under my arm like a football.

The bartender nodded approvingly. "Now, keep that brown bag under your table. That's the law 'round these parts."

We sipped our drinks, feeling mighty pleased with ourselves for navigating the local customs. After a spell, Billy piped up, "Say, you know where a couple of fellas might find some dancing and pretty girls?"

The bartender pointed us to a joint upstairs. We climbed the twenty-five steps, our precious cargo safely stowed under the table once more.

Now, I don't know if it was the unfamiliar surroundings or the Seagram's talking, but before long, we found ourselves mingling with the locals. Billy, smooth operator that he was, soon had himself a dance partner and an invitation to join a table of girls.

Me? I ended up shooting the breeze with some local college boys. They were going on about some jazz club we just had to check out.

"Hey, Billy," I called over, "I'm gonna check out this other place with the fellas. I'll be back in a jiffy."

Now, I'd like to say I made it down the stairs with the grace of Fred Astaire. Truth is, I took two steps before my knee gave out, and I tumbled down the stairs like a sack of potatoes. Thank the Lord I had that hotel calling card in my pocket, 'cause the next thing I remember is waking up in our hotel room. The sun was shining through the window over my bed, and I felt like I'd gone ten rounds with a grizzly bear. I had a hard time figuring out where I had slept.

Billy stumbled in sometime later, looking like the cat who ate the canary. His eyes went wide when he saw me.

"Jim, you look like you tangled with a barbed wire fence and lost! Better get yourself cleaned up."

I dragged myself to the mirror, and Lord have mercy, I was a sight! Blood caked down the side of my face where my glasses had done a number on me. Speaking of which, one lens was hanging on by a prayer.

After a shower and emergency repairs with scotch tape courtesy of the desk clerk, we hit the road. But our luck seemed to have run dry. Cars whizzed by, ignoring our outstretched thumbs.

Finally, Billy turned to me. "Jim, no offense, but you look like death warmed over. Why don't you take a load off in the ditch there? I'll holler when we get a ride."

So there I was, nursing my wounds in a Tennessee ditch, wondering how I was gonna explain this to my roommates back on campus.

Before long, Billy's voice roused me from my pity party. Another kind soul had stopped for us—another salesman, as luck would have it.

Now, I don't know if you've ever been in a car with a parent, but let me tell you, that fella had the dad reflex down pat. When he had to slam on the brakes in town, his right arm shot out faster than greased lightning, catching me square in the chest.

"Sorry 'bout that," he said, looking sheepish. "Force of habit from riding with my kids."

I wheezed out a laugh. "No harm done, sir. Reckon it's good to know someone's looking out for us."

The rest of the journey home was a blur of kind strangers and dwindling ham sandwiches. By the time we hit St. Joseph, we were running on fumes—both literally and figuratively.

We splurged on a motel room; our travels having taught us the value of a good night's sleep. Come morning, we caught a city bus through St. Joseph, then hit Highway 36 with our thumbs out once more.

Four rides later, we finally saw the "Welcome to Lincoln" sign. I coulda kissed the ground, I was so happy to be home.

"Billy," I said, as we stood on the side of Highway 77, "I reckon this is one spring break I won't soon forget."

Billy laughed, hefting our suitcase full of dirty laundry. "You can say that again. Mama's sandwiches are long gone, but we've got stories to last a lifetime."

I fished out a dime and found a pay phone, ringing up my roommate Dale.

"Hey, Dale? It's Jim. Mind coming to fetch a couple of weary travelers?"

As we waited for our ride, I reflected on the journey we'd had. From the kindness of Mr. Steele to the perils of Nashville stairs, it had been one heck of an adventure.

Billy must've been thinking the same thing. "You know, Jim," he said, "I reckon we've seen the best of folks on this trip. Makes a fella proud to be part of the human race."

I nodded, thinking of all the strangers who'd gone out of their way to help us.

"You're right about that, Billy. Reckon there's a lot more good in this world than we sometimes remember."

As Dale's car pulled up, I knew we'd be telling these stories for years to come. Spring break might've been over, but the memories? Well, they were just getting started.

Chapter 33: From Cornhusker Country to Tobacco Roads

It was hotter than a firecracker that summer when Ed Johnson came up to me, grinning like a possum eating persimmons.

"Hey Jim," he said, "got a message for ya. Billy Childers called. Says to give him a ring when you get a chance."

I raised an eyebrow. "Billy from Hickory? Now that's a blast from the past."

When I called Billy back, his voice crackled with excitement over the line. "Jim! How'd you like to come down to Hickory for the summer? I've got some wild plans, and I could use a wingman."

"Wild plans, huh?" I chuckled. "Alright, count me in. When should I head down?"

"Yesterday!" Billy laughed. "But seriously, come on down whenever you can. We'll have a grand old time."

So there I was, packing a suitcase with the bare essentials. Ed offered to give me a lift to Superior, Nebraska, close to the Missouri border.

"You sure about this hitchhiking business?" Ed asked as we pulled up to the highway. "It's a long way to North Carolina."

I grinned, holding up my makeshift sign. "Adventure waits for no man, Ed. Besides, I've got my wits and this fancy piece of cardboard. What could go wrong?"

Ed shook his head, smiling. "Alright, cowboy. Just don't end up in a ditch somewhere."

The first few rides were a breeze. In St. Joseph, Missouri, I hopped on a city bus. The driver eyed me curiously.

"Where you headed, son?" he asked.

"Hickory, North Carolina," I replied proudly.

He let out a low whistle. "Well, you've got a ways to go. Good luck to ya."

By noon, I'd made it to Interstate 70. A salesman in a shiny Buick picked me up.

"St. Louis, eh?" he said, eyeing my sign. "Hop in. I can take you all the way across Missouri."

As we cruised down the highway, he regaled me with tales of life on the road.

"You know," he said, glancing at me, "there's nothing like seeing the country this way. Every day's an adventure."

I nodded, thinking to myself, "Ain't that the truth."

The next morning, I found myself on a quiet stretch of Interstate 64. Just as I started to wonder if I'd made a mistake, an old pickup with a camper came chugging along.

The driver, an old-timer with a cigar clamped between his teeth, stopped right in the middle of the freeway.

"Son," he called out, "where you headed?"

"Hickory, North Carolina, sir," I replied, a bit taken aback.

He grinned, revealing a gold tooth. "Well, I'm headed to Lexington, Kentucky. Climb on up here."

As we rolled along, he introduced himself as Henry and started chatting like we were old friends.

"Say, you ever seen a real tobacco farm?" he asked.

I shook my head. "Can't say that I have, sir. Only in magazine ads."

"Well, we're gonna change that today," he declared. "But first, how about some lunch at my place? I've got a bit of history I'd like to show you."

Henry's house turned out to be a grand old mansion. As we walked in, one entire wall in the kitchen was covered with framed pictures of high-stepping horses. Henry began telling me that his granddaughter loved horses, and she was going to ride in a show tonight. He proceeded making sandwiches along with iced tea.

He then said, "I want you to stay overnight and go with me to see my granddaughter's show. Are you in a hurry to get to North Carolina?"

I told him I had a friend waiting for me and I had to be in Hickory before nightfall because it's hard to get a ride when it gets dark at night.

The next item on his agenda was to have me go upstairs and see his bedroom. As we were walking up the stairs he said his grandfather was the governor of Kentucky at one time. He pointed to a four-poster bed which had a canopy over the top. Then he said, "Abraham Lincoln would come to stay with my grandfather and slept in this bed overnight. See that?" he said proudly. "Ol' Abe Lincoln himself slept there."

My jaw dropped. "No kidding? That's something else!"

Over ham sandwiches, Henry regaled me with stories of his family's history. Then he took me out to see his tobacco farm.

As we walked through the fields, Henry turned to me. "You know, son, life's full of unexpected detours. Sometimes they turn out to be the best part of the journey."

I nodded, thinking how right he was.

The rest of the trip was a whirlwind. In Asheville, I got caught in a rainstorm. A family in a station wagon pulled over, their little boy's face pressed against the window.

"Daddy, look!" the boy exclaimed. "It's a real-life hitchhiker!"

The father chuckled. "Hop in, son. We're headed to Hickory ourselves."

When I finally made it to Hickory, it was pitch dark. Billy and his girlfriend Hannah were waiting for me at a local diner.

"Jim!" Billy hollered, slapping me on the back. "You made it! How was the trip?"

I grinned. "Let's just say it was an adventure."

***

The next morning, Billy shook me awake at the crack of dawn. "Rise and shine, sleeping beauty! We've got papers to deliver!"

As we tossed newspapers from his station wagon, Billy filled me in on his summer gig.

"So get this," he said, excitement in his voice. "I'm repossessing cars for the loan company. It's like being a secret agent, but with more angry people and less martinis."

I raised an eyebrow. "Sounds...interesting. And potentially dangerous."

Billy laughed. "Nah, it's a piece of cake. You'll see tonight when you come along as my lookout."

That night, as he crept up to a house with a car scheduled for repossession, I whispered because he left the getaway car which I was supposed to be driving, "Billy, are you sure about this?"

He grinned in the darkness. "Trust me, it'll be fine. Just keep the engine running and follow me when I do get the car to be repossessed."

Every morning I would go with Billy to deliver newspapers. I then drove the backup car as Billy repossessed cars that people were not making payments on.

Two weeks passed, and I found myself looking for steadier work. I landed a job at the local carpet mill, making floor mats for Chevy cars.

My supervisor, a gruff man named Bob, showed me the ropes. "It ain't glamorous," he said, "but it's honest work, twelve hours a day, six days a week. You'll be making $55 a week."

As summer wound down, Billy's brother gifted Billy his old car which was parked in Mom's garage. "Ready for a road trip back to Lincoln?" Billy asked.

I nodded, ready to head home but grateful for the summer's adventures.

***

The next morning, I dragged myself out of bed, still bone-tired from yesterday's trip with Billy from Hickory in his brother's car. As I shuffled into the kitchen, my roommate Gary was already there, cuppa joe in hand.

"Morning, sunshine," he drawled. "Ready for another exciting day of learning?"

I grunted in response, pouring myself some coffee. "About as ready as a turkey on Thanksgiving."

This was my senior year, and I had my classes lined up and scheduled around my work at the University Club with June.

We both chuckled as we headed out to class. The morning flew by in a haze of lectures and note-taking. Before I knew it, the clock struck noon, and I was hightailing it over to the University Club for my shift.

As I tied on my apron, my supervisor, June, gave me a sympathetic look. "You look like you've been rode hard and put away wet, hon. Rough night?"

I shook my head, smiling. "Nah, just the usual. Burning the candle at both ends. You know how it is."

The lunch crowd kept us hopping until 2 o'clock. I barely had time to catch my breath before I was back in class, my mind already on the dinner shift ahead.

Five o'clock rolled around, and I was back at the Club, greeting the regulars with a smile and a "How y'all doing this fine evening?"

Old Mr. Johnson, a retired professor who came in every night, patted my arm. "You're a good kid, working so hard. Don't forget to take care of yourself, ya hear?"

I nodded, touched by his concern. "Yes sir, I'm doing my best."

The dinner rush finally died down around 8:00 p.m., and I settled in for my nightly routine of studying and homework. The quiet hum of the Club was a comfort as I pored over my books.

At 11 o'clock, I locked up, my brain full to bursting with facts and figures. This was my life, day in and day out, but you know what? I wouldn't have had it any other way.

Before I knew it, the school year was over, and I had enough credits to graduate. I couldn't believe it—Jimmy Brown, orphan boy, about to get my degree from the University of Nebraska!

I wanted to thank everyone who'd helped me along the way, so I sent out announcements with a little poem I'd cooked up. It went something like this:

Thanks For The

Gifts: I need none—
for the helping hand you gave
is the thing I will always save.
Praise: I need none—
for all the encouragement I have had along the way
has kept me from going astray.
Homes: I need none—
for wherever I go I will always feel
that I am one of you
for you have gone out of your way
to make pleasure out of my stay.
Thanks is all I need—
for I cannot find enough of these
to let you know how much I am pleased
to be a product of your kindnesses.
—James Brown

As I sealed the last envelope, I felt a swell of pride. It hadn't been easy, but with a little determination and a whole lot of help from my friends and family, I'd done it taking six years to get through four years at the University. I was ready to face whatever came next, armed with my education, and a heart full of gratitude.

Chapter 34: Everyone Loves a Sweet Ending, Right?

One sultry afternoon, as I was wiping down the bar for the umpteenth time, Mr. Thompson, the manager of the University Club, called me into his office. The air conditioning was on the fritz again, and I could see beads of sweat forming on his forehead as I walked in.

"Jim, my boy," he said, leaning back in his creaky chair that had seen better days, "June tells me you've been helping her turn more revenue in the bar this year. Says the clients can't get enough of ya."

I felt my cheeks go red as a Nebraska sunset. "Aw, shucks, Pete. I'm just doing my best."

"Well, your best is mighty fine," he chuckled, his belly shaking like Santa Claus. "So, what's next for our star bartender?"

I shuffled my feet a bit, suddenly finding the worn carpet mighty interesting. "Well, sir, I gotta attend a physics class this summer. But I'd like to keep working here at the club till I'm through with that. I've really enjoyed my time here, and June's just the bee's knees to work with."

Mr. Thompson's eyes lit up like a firefly on a warm July night. "Say, that reminds me. The club and I, we'd like to celebrate your graduation. How 'bout we throw you and your folks a little shindig here? A graduation day luncheon, what do you say?"

I was so touched, I nearly choked up. It was moments like these that reminded me why I loved this place so darn much.

"That's mighty kind of you, Mr. Thompson. I'd be honored."

"Excellent!" he said and clapped his hands, the sound echoing in the small office. "You just make up a list of who you want there. Your kin, of course, and any friends who helped you through school. Let me know how many and when, and we'll make it happen."

As I left Mr. Thompson's office, my mind was whirling like a tornado in spring. I'd done it—graduated college. But now what? It felt like I'd walked the plank, and now I had to jump into the water and start swimming. What was gonna be my next big adventure?

That's when I remembered all those late-night chats with George Sullivan, the trainer for the Cornhuskers. He'd put a bug in my ear about becoming a trainer for a professional football team. Said most of 'em weren't college educated or medically trained, and that I should consider being a physical therapist first.

"Jim," he'd told me one night after a grueling game, "you've got a real gift for this. Don't waste it. Go get yourself some proper training, and you could really make a difference."

So, with George's help, I applied to a handful of colleges with physical therapy programs. Got responses from some big names like Hermann Medical Hospital in Texas and the Mayo Clinic in Minnesota. Both said if I could complete a physics course, I'd be in like Flynn.

So there I was, working at the University Club and sweating through summer school, trying to get that physics credit. Halfway through, I was struggling like a cat in a bathtub. The formulas and equations swam before my eyes, making about as much sense as a cow on roller skates.

I went to the teacher, hat in hand, asking for a tutor.

"Ma'am," I said, my voice shaking more than I'd like to admit, "I need to get a B in this class to get into the physical therapy program. Could you help me out?"

She set me up with a tutor, a skinny kid named Ernie who looked like he'd been born with a calculator in his hand. I worked my tail off, studying late into the night after my shifts at the club. Ernie was patient, explaining things over and over until they finally made sense.

But when the final grades came in, I'd only managed a C+. My heart sank like a stone in a still pond.

I went back to the professor, praying she'd have mercy. "Ma'am," I pleaded, my voice barely above a whisper, "I've applied to Mayo Clinic. Without a B in this class, I can't attend the program. Is there anything I can do?"

She looked at me with eyes cold as a winter morning. "I'm sorry, but I cannot increase your grade. It wouldn't be fair to the rest of the class."

I felt like I'd been punched in the gut by the biggest linebacker in the league. "So you're telling me I can't pursue my dream of being a physical therapist because you won't change my grade?"

"That's the way it is," she said, firm as an old oak. "You didn't earn the B grade."

I walked out of that physics building feeling like a balloon with all the air let out. The sun was shining, birds were singing, but to me, the world had never looked so gray. Didn't know what I was gonna do with my life now. So, I went back to the University Club and kept on bartending for a couple weeks, trying to figure out my next move.

The regulars could tell something was off. Old Mr. Johnson, who'd been coming to the club since before I was born, cornered me one night.

"Jim, my boy," he said, his voice gravelly with age, "what's eating at you? You look like you've lost your best friend."

I spilled the whole story, the words tumbling out like a river after a spring thaw. When I finished, Mr. Johnson was quiet for a long moment, swirling the ice in his glass.

"You know," he said finally, "I've lived a long time, and if there's one thing I've learned, it's that life rarely goes according to plan. But that doesn't mean it can't be wonderful."

He leaned in close, his eyes twinkling. "When one door closes, another opens. You just gotta keep your eyes peeled for it."

As I pondered Mr. Johnson's words over the next few days, I realized he was right. Maybe being a physical therapist wasn't in the cards for me, but that didn't mean my life was over. I'd graduated college, hadn't I? That was something my relatives, along with some back- home friends never thought they'd see.

And as I looked around the University Club, at the people I knew and cared for over the years, I realized something else. I was good at this. Not just mixing drinks, but talking to people, making them feel welcome and heard. Maybe there was something to that.

***

A week after my graduation dinner at the Club, along with my graduation exercise, I'd barely settled into my old routine when I got a call from George Sullivan at the University.

"Jim," he said, "how would you feel about a trainer job down in Odessa, Texas?"

My first question was, "Where is Odessa and how many miles is it to get there?"

George said, "Odessa is maybe a two-day drive."

George then said, "The administrator wanted someone there as soon as possible. Are you interested?"

I asked, "What is the pay scale?"

George asked me to get a pencil to write down the administrator's phone number.

"Call him in the next hour and get all your question answered. Then you can make up your mind."

I thanked George for the information and then hung up. I paused, thinking about all I'd experienced that summer. I wrote down some questions for the administrator and called Mr. Fisher twenty minutes later. He answered my questions and gave me information about teaching and the salary which were very interesting.

As I hung up the phone, I smiled. Life sure had a funny way of keeping things interesting. I called Mr. Fisher the next day and told him I would take the job, and I'd arrive in Odessa in two days.

And you know what? I wouldn't change a thing. That physics class I thought had ruined everything? It taught me one of the most valuable lessons of my life: failure isn't the end, it's just a detour. Every setback is a setup for a comeback.

So if you're reading this and feeling lost, like your dreams are slipping away, remember my story. Keep your chin up and your eyes open. Your path might not be the one you planned, but that doesn't mean it can't lead you somewhere wonderful. After all, life's not about the destination, it's about the journey. And what a journey it's been.

Acknowledgments

Writing this book brought back a lot of memories of what it was like to be part of a community that cares for their youth. As I cherished the thoughts of my young life, I knew I wanted to leave a legacy for my family and friends.

I am deeply grateful to Candace Sinclair for her guidance and encouragement in helping me put my experiences into a story. Her support was invaluable in allowing me to share how it is possible to earn a college degree with the help of many caring friends and supporters. I could not have completed this journey without Candace's mentorship and belief in my ability to succeed.

Thanks to the people who gave me advice, encouragement, and who carried for my being: George Sullivan, June Kruger, Auntie Beth, and Maryellen Lorton.

I especially want to thank my wife, Charlotte Moncato, for over fifty years of growing and guidance, for she was the angel who came into my life.

About the Author

James Brown lives in Huntington Beach, California with his wife, Charlotte. He is a retired physical therapist who spent fifty-one years treating patients in his multiple offices and through contracts with rehab agencies for at-home patients. He and his wife have two grown sons, five grandsons, and one granddaughter. This is the third book in the three-book series about Jimmy Brown.

You can visit the Jimmy Brown Club website to learn more about new releases and to view photos and a video of Jimmy's childhood: www.jimmybrownclub.com[1].

---

1.   http://www.jimmybrownclub.com

About the Author

About the Author

James Brown lives in Huntington Beach, California with his wife, Charlotte. He is a retired physical therapist who spent fifty-one years treating patients in his multiple offices and through contracts with rehab agencies for at-home patients. He and his wife have two grown sons, five grandsons, and one granddaughter. This is the third book in the three-book series about Jimmy Brown.

You can visit the Jimmy Brown Club website to learn more about new releases and to view photos and a video of Jimmy's childhood: .

Read more at www.jimmybrownclub.com.